SHORT CUTS

INTRODUCTIONS TO FILM STUDIES

OTHER TITLES IN THE SHORT CUTS SERIES

FEMINIST FILM STUDIES

WRITING THE WOMAN INTO CINEMA

JANET McCABE

WALLFLOWER

LONDON and NEW YORK

A Wallflower Paperback

First published in Great Britain in 2004 by
Wallflower Press
4th Floor, 26 Shacklewell Lane, London E8 2EZ
www.wallflowerpress.co.uk

A catalogue record for this book is available from the British Library

ISBN 1 904764-03-7

Book Design by Rob Bowden Design

Printed in Great Britain by Antony Rowe Ltd, Chippenham, Wiltshire

CONTENTS

ACKNOWLEDGEMENTS

Let me first express my thanks to the students at the University of North London who took my 'Women's Cinema' classes between 1996 and 2001, and for asking difficult questions and generating stimulating debate.

Grateful thanks to Wallflower Press, and especially to Yoram Allon for believing that the manuscript would finally appear.

Finally, my deepest gratitude goes to Kim Akass and Mike Allen for reading the various drafts with interest and great care.

The book is dedicated with love to my mother – Elizabeth McCabe

INTRODUCTION: WOMAN IS NOT BORN BUT BECOMES A WOMAN

This book charts the development of feminist film theory and the theorising of cinema in relation to the issues raised by feminist inquiry from the early 1970s to the present. The broad range of know-ledges produced by film feminism is quite extraordinary, dependent upon different aims, objectives and intellectual interests. This introduction aims to document this dynamic critical field of feminist film studies – to chart the numerous feminist interventions and to critically think about how the socio-historical, political and cultural contexts shaped what was said and how it was said.

The body of work called feminist film theory and criticism has played a crucial – and often controversial – role in the emergence of film studies as an academic discipline; in turn, film studies shaped feminist concerns as well as granted feminist research a space to flourish. Demonstrating an awareness of the origins and influences that shape feminist film theory may help us rethink our ideas about how a field of knowledge is determined. In knowing how film feminism formed, we may also learn what it wants us to know and how individual theoretical texts fit into a larger field of study. Feminist film theory is a very particular type of theory, conceived from disciplines beyond its borders such as (post)structuralism, psychoanalysis, post-colonialism and queer theory as well as generated from inside film studies. Studying the field of knowledge known as feminist film studies allows us to read it as a set of statements about the institution of cinema and cultural production, about representational categories and gendered subjectivity, about identification and spectatorship practices, about cultural authority and historical (in)visibility, about desire and fantasy, and about the interaction between these areas.

Feminist film theory and criticism has contributed enormously to our understanding on sexual difference and gender identity. Writers and thinkers working in this area over time have developed new critical methodologies and theories, producing new knowledges concerned with deconstructing representation and offering new statements within which, and by which, the woman, either as subject or object, can be known. Authors challenged orthodox theories and film histories, to rethink representational categories as well as reclaim the contribution made by women to the history of cinema and filmmaking practice. In recent years, feminist film research extended its cultural interests and influence. Interrogating representations of race, ethnic identity and class in relation to gender allowed scholars to broaden the film feminism remit. Turning to other media such as television and video also gave academics an opportunity to expand thinking, and to reconsider film historiography, most notably in relation to consumer culture and historicising film reception and exhibition, further stretched the field. Interest in popular culture resulted in shifting attention away from textual analysis and theories of the subject to broader cultural issues concerned with industrial practices, institutional strategies and audiences. Postmodernity, globalisation and transnationalism, digital technologies and new medias continue to pose fresh questions for film feminism and raise new methodological challenges for the discipline.

I take the critical work of the first feminist scholars as my starting point. Conceived in the politically radical context of the women's liberation movement, and at an historical moment when women in Western Europe and America lobbied for improved political representation and sexual equality, the emergence of feminist film theory and criticism drew strength from this liberal, left-wing political struggle. The socio-cultural construct of femininity, long discussed by women thinkers dating back to Mary Wollstonecraft (1759–97), was identified as the primary source of female political oppression, economic subordination and historical invisibility. Second-wave feminism, defined by Annette Kuhn, is broadly 'a set of political practices founded in analyses of the social/historical position of women as subordinated, oppressed or exploited either within dominant modes of production [such as capitalism] and/or by the social relations of patriarchy or male domination' (1985: 4). Raising awareness about how patriarchal ideology excluded, silenced and oppressed women would indelibly mark this political movement.

Early feminist initiatives into film theory in the 1970s were framed by two other feminist interventions: the history of second-wave feminism and theoretical accounts that deal with images of women created and circulated within our dominant culture defined by patriarchy and heterosexuality. It is to these antecedents – what Laura Mulvey called the 'wider explosive meeting between feminism and patriarchal culture' (1979: 3) – that I turn to first in order to contextualise the earliest feminist writings on film.

Simone de Beauvoir and The Second Sex

What laid the foundation for the political and theoretical work undertaken in the early 1970s was Simone de Beauvoir's account of why Woman is defined as 'Other':

> One is not born, but rather becomes, a woman. No biological, psychological, or economic fate determines the figure that the human female presents in society; it is civilisation as a whole that produces this creature, intermediate between male and eunuch, which is described as feminine. Only the intervention of someone else can establish an individual as an *Other*. (1984: 295)

De Beauvoir's treaty on the myth of woman as Other is grounded in the existentialist ethics set out by Jean-Paul Sartre, in which he argued that human freedom is achieved through a constant state of action (or, transcendence). Existentialist theory suggests that there is no divine justification for existence other than the need to self-justify one's own being. The subject, existing in a perpetual state of self-awareness and self-analysis, achieves transcendence by actively shifting away from a state of passivity and stagnation (or, immanence). Reframing these ideas, de Beauvoir genderises transcendence and immanence, to suggest that the Self can only be determined with reference to what it is not. Man therefore proceeds to confirm the woman as Other in the process of identifying himself as Subject.

> She is defined and differentiated with reference to man and not he with reference to her; she is the incidental, the inessential as

3

opposed to the essential. He is the Subject, he is the Absolute
– she is the Other. (1984: 16)

Woman verifies male transcendence; she is the object against which the
male must differentiate himself to attain subjectivity.

Finding no compelling reason in the fields of natural science or
psychoanalysis for explaining why the woman should be biologically
inferior suggested to de Beauvoir that patriarchal culture is somehow
responsible for generating and circulating self-confirming parameters
that institute gender hierarchies and sexual inequalities. The female
emerges as condemned to her subordinate role, 'defined exclusively in
her relation to man' (1984: 174). For this reason, cultural constructions of
woman possess no stable meaning, argues de Beauvoir: 'she is a false
Infinite, an Ideal without truth' (1984: 218). Patriarchal knowledge instead
relentlessly constructs an idea of woman as a projection of male fantasies
and anxieties, of phallocentric Otherness and masculine lack. What is
more, these ideals translate into virile myths of the unattainable ('she is
all that man desires and all that he does not attain' (1984: 229)), of ideal
beauty and perfection, of Death and abjection ('the hero lost for ever as he
falls back into the maternal shadows – cave, abyss, hell' (1984: 179)).

> She is an idol, a servant, the source of life, a power of darkness;
> she is the elemental silence of truth, she is artifice, gossip and
> falsehood; she is healing presence and sorceress; she is man's
> prey, his downfall, she is everything that he is not and that he
> longs for, his negation and his *raison d'être*. (1984: 175)

The eternal feminine myth emerges as nothing more than a patriarchal
construction, representing both everything and nothing, ideal and
monstrous.

No gendered body exists that has not already been inscribed with, and
interpreted by, cultural meanings, argues de Beauvoir. Social myths are
transmitted through culture – 'religions, traditions, language, tales, songs,
movies' (1984: 290) – which in turn constructs how the individual comes
to know, perceive and experience the material world. Yet, 'representation
of the world ... is the work of men' which depicts it 'from their own point of
view' and is confused 'with absolute truth' (1984: 175). Such is the vigour
of the patriarchal discourse that myths, theories, opinions, philosophies

generated over centuries regarding gender hierarchies and sexual inequalities assume the status of received wisdom: 'proving woman's inferiority [draws] not only upon religion, philosophy and theology … but also upon science – biology, experimental psychology' (1984: 23); and it is through these discourses, contends de Beauvoir, that women learn to be object rather than subject: 'the "true woman" is required to make herself object, to be the Other' (1984: 291).

Second-wave feminism and feminist interventions

De Beauvoir's existentialist account of woman as Other initiated debate as second-wave feminists, keen to understand the roots of female oppression, addressed the various implications of her thinking, as it seemed to offer an explanation to the roots of female oppression. Betty Friedan, for example, revises de Beauvoir's ideas of transcendence within an American socio-cultural context that promotes self-determinism and personal fulfilment as a right for all citizens: 'this is the crisis of women growing up – a turning point from an immaturity that has been called femininity to full human identity' (1965: 70). Friedan describes the 'feminine mystique' as a discourse seeking to identify the 'truth' about 'natural' feminine roles, only 'find femininity in sexual passivity, male domination, and nurturing maternal love' (1965: 38).

Friedan charts how the latest incarnation of the 'feminine mystique' adapts the virgin/whore dichotomy that has long defined dominant images of the female. This divide in American post-war culture is between housewife and career woman, she argues. Looking at images of contemporary femininity found in popular culture, from print journalism to film representation and star discourses, enables her to claim that the 'feminine mystique' socialises women into willingly accepting roles as wives and mothers without question:

> But by then the new image of American woman, 'Occupation: housewife', had hardened into a mystique, unquestioned and permitting no questions, shaping the very reality it distorted. (1965: 44)

So powerful are these cultural images that women no longer knew who they were. Emancipation is possible, contends Friedan, if cultural images are 'reshaped' and women educated 'to reach maturity, identity, completeness of self without conflict with sexual fulfilment' (1965: 318). Nowhere does she offer a theoretical framework for deconstructing ideology, and neither does she understand the complex processes at work in producing the representations she describes. Yet her important link between the power of the image and women's material existence ignited further discussion.

Second-wave feminist theoretical works such as Shulamith Firestone's *The Dialectic of Sex*, Eva Figes' *Patriarchal Attitudes* and Germaine Greer's *Female Eunuch*, all originally published in 1970, stressed the politics of culture. Kate Millett in particular takes up the issue of female oppression under patriarchy in *Sexual Politics* (also 1970). Noting first how patriarchy prevails not through coercion but consent, she argues how women are socialised into accepting an inferior social status. Tracing how cultural articulations of patriarchy, from ancient mythology to contemporary scientific theories, inscribe the ideology of femininity prompts her to draw parallels between political and legal disenfranchisement (campaigns for abortion rights), acts committed against the female body such as rape, sexual harassment and domestic violence, and how cultural forms, like pornography, confirm female objectification.

These pioneering studies underpinned the radical political action of the feminist movement, offering knowledge about how the patriarchal world worked to oppress women. Drawing directly on de Beauvoir's work allowed second-wave feminist writers to propose uncompromising cultural histories of female oppression, sexual inequality and gender exclusion: 'culture is so saturated with male bias that women almost never have a chance to see themselves culturally through their own eyes' (Firestone 1979: 149). These writings not only proved useful for deconstructing patriarchal ideology in which the supremacy and importance of male subjectivity had gone unquestioned, but also identified new spaces for female resistance and the articulation of an alternative, subjective feminine experience. As an identifiable area by the 1970s, feminist theory gave voice to a female political consciousness in which the 'personal *is* political'.

Second-wave feminism and film criticism.

Early feminist inquiries into images of women on film shared a similar agenda as those writing on the politics of representation. Stereotypical images of women and the female body on film came under close scrutiny as critics and scholars looked at how best to interpret gender and representation in relation to patriarchy. Initial feminist interventions into understanding the ways in which women are depicted on film aimed to expose the sexist content of cinema narratives as well as how the media constructs women as sex objects. An engagement with the investigation of what Mary Ann Doane, Patricia Mellencamp and Linda Williams (1984) referred to as 'images of women' will be used here to sketch out the key issues discussed by feminist film studies as well as describe the chapter-by-chapter structure of this book.

Much of what might be called the first attempt at devising a feminist film criticism focuses on female representation as somehow reflecting real social attitudes, opinions, cultural values and patriarchal myths:

> Women were ... the barometers of changing fashion. Like two-way mirrors linking the immediate past with the immediate future, women in the movies reflected, perpetuated, and in some respects offered innovations of the roles of women in society. (Haskell 1987: 12)

Molly Haskell and Marjorie Rosen's historical studies on the treatment of women in the movies are generally considered good examples of what is commonly referred to as 'reflection theory'. Both accounts propose uncompromising feminist critiques of how Hollywood cinema has over time repressed women through categorising female types in film: the glamour goddess, the *femme fatale*, the self-sacrificing mother. Another sociological approach came from Joan Mellen (1974) with her account of the sexist structures at work in European cinema. Grounding each contribution is the underlying assumption that films somehow hold up a reflective mirror to society; as Haskell declares in her introduction: 'Movies are one of the clearest and most accessible of looking glasses into the past, being both cultural artefacts and mirrors' (1987: xviii).

Rosen's cultural history chronicling the changing image of the ideal Hollywood woman owes as much to de Beauvoir's formulation of the eternal feminine myth as it does to Friedan's thinking on socio-cultural constructions of women in *The Feminine Mystique*. *Popcorn Venus* traces how Hollywood shaped its female stars and assembled its film narratives against the backdrop of seismic social and economic changes taking place in twentieth-century America, as 'the industry held a warped mirror up to life' (1973: 81).

Hollywood is understood by Rosen as an institution geared toward the production of patriarchal ideology and a powerful carrier of its values and ideas. Drawing explicitly on de Beauvoir's ideas of how patriarchal cultural myths govern human perception allows Rosen to identify how film versions of femininity speak of male cultural dominance, images which in turn are offered to real women to identify with and/or adopt. These stereotypical images afford female audiences little chance for authentic recognition. Instead they produce a false consciousness for women, offering them nothing but an escape into fantasy through identification with stereotypical images: 'How profoundly Hollywood's values have influenced a gullible public – like myself. But why did the public – and especially its females – so passively embrace the industry's interpretation of life?' (1973: 9). Despite generating new representations that coincided with real advancements made by women, the industry's continual depiction of women as sex objects or victims suggests to Rosen that these images spoke of patriarchal anxieties regarding the loss of male socio-economic and sexual power.

Nowhere is the site of struggle over social change and cultural representation so evident as in the figure of female stars, 'our Popcorn Venuses' (1973: 388). Aligned with the character she plays, the star embodies patriarchal fantasies while eliminating male fears, 'celluloid aphrodisiacs – talking, walking and comforting a patriarchal society' (1973: 154). Yet, in being forced to live out on-screen fantasies off-screen, the women behind the icon contest and subvert what their image exemplifies to reveal contradiction. Defining the star as reflecting and misrepresenting the real leads Rosen to make an important link between text and context, in which the female star emerges as a site of contestation.

Haskell's *From Reverence to Rape* is an equally uncompromising view of American cinema and its depiction of women. She narrativises the decade-by-decade shift in female representation as an arc from 'reverence' (the silent era) to 'rape' (Hollywood in the 1960s and 1970s): 'As the propaganda arm of the American Dream machine', and paralleling the real socio-political changes for women, the American film industry 'manoeuvred to keep women in their place' (1987: 2, 3). Hollywood produced female 'myths of subjection and sacrifice' (1987: 3), from the 'Victorian virgins' of the 1910s and 1920s to the deified sex goddesses and 'sultry (and diabolical) *femmes fatales* of traditional male fantasy' (1987: 374). Veneration increasingly turns to sexual violence and misogyny during the liberated 1960s. The reason for this reactive response is clear argues Haskell: 'The growing strength and demands of women in real life, spearheaded by women's liberation, obviously provoked a backlash in commercial film' (1987: 323).

Haskell's argument proves more complex than the trajectory of her reverence to rape thesis initially suggests. She begins by echoing de Beauvoir's thinking on how Western culture embeds women's inferiority into its social fabric:

> The big lie perpetrated in Western society is the idea of women's inferiority, a lie so deeply ingrained in our social behaviour that merely to recognise it is to risk unravelling the entire fabric of civilisation. (1987: 1)

Hollywood, as 'an industry dedicated for the most part of reinforcing the lie' (1987: 2), generates and continues to perpetuate ideas of how the woman is perceived by society.

Suggesting that cinema has historically functioned to mask female achievement and promote the male point of view prompts her to concentrate on the ways in which Hollywood movies simultaneously reproduce social realities while distorting women's experience of those realities. Yet film, she argues, represents neither a conscious conspiracy nor a particular ideological stance. Unconscious drives and cultural repression, working at a much deeper level, instead determine how women are represented on screen. Contradiction and social taboo further condition these images of an ideologically laden femininity. Her quasi-sociological approach tentatively suggests how film meaning is made by the obsessions, both conscious and unconscious, of its director as well as by other dissident opinions. Competing voices belonging more often than not to the female stars like Bette Davis and Barbara Stanwyck expose the internal contradictions at work within the text but also those involved in the making of a star. 'The personality of the star, the mere fact of being a star, was as important as the roles they played, and affected the very conception of those roles' (1987: 5). Stanwyck may step into the stock feminine role of 'lower-class woman as martyr' in King Vidor's 1937 film *Stella Dallas* but her 'excruciating and exhilarating performance ... takes Stella onto a [different] plane where she ... breaks our hearts even as she grates on our nerves' (ibid.). What Haskell suggests here is that Stanwyck brings something else to the role while contesting the feminine stereotype she portrays in the process.

Haskell and Rosen contributed a great deal to initial feminist understanding of how representation is intricately linked to patriarchal myths, values and opinions: 'Woman's image of herself is so entwined in the tangle of myths and inventions made by man that it is hard to look at it straight' (Haskell 1987: 278). But their claim that cinema reduces images of women to a limited range of female stereotypes as a 'vehicle of male fantasies' and 'the scapegoat of men's fears' (1987: 40) is never proved beyond listing historical examples and sweeping claims. These writers, while recognising the ability of the film image to naturalise what is only a projection of patriarchal ideology, were seen by other feminists as failing to provide adequate theoretical frameworks for deconstructing the complexity of what they were saying. Their theoretical assumption, founded upon the second-wave feminist presupposition of a direct relation between representation and social values fixed by ideology, could not – in the opinion of Claire Johnston, Pam Cook and others – sufficiently account for how ideology functions to produce meaning *within* the film text.

Images do not simply reflect the social world but are ideological signifiers. Chapter one, 'Structuring a Language of Theory', explores the intellectual activities of feminist film scholars, critics and filmmakers, coming out of Britain in the 1970s, in formulating a theory of film from a feminist bias. Theorists turned to (post)structuralism, continental philosophy and psychoanalysis to address the perceived theoretical lack as well as to identify critical methods and conceptual tools that could be used to formulate a feminist film theory. Those who provided terms and debates acted upon film theory to advance a feminist methodology while legitimising its frame of reference and intellectual standpoint. Such work revealed that women had no easy access to her own voice in the phallocentrism of semiotics and psychoanalysis; but in the writing of the new feminist film theory discourse, scholars nevertheless struggled to construct a new theoretical language with which to speak by interrogating the very methods they had appropriated or adopted. Put simply, feminist scholars interrogated the appropriateness of using psychoanalysis in the very process of revising it for feminist film theory.

Feminists from cultural studies would in turn point to the limits of the semiotic-psychoanalytic theoretical project. Theirs instead was a debate about text and context anticipated earlier by Haskell in her useful

– if uneasy – intervention related to representation and its reception. This argument is most fully developed in her chapter on the 'woman's film' of the 1930s and 1940s:

> Because the woman's film was designed for and tailored to a certain market, its recurrent themes represent the closest thing to an expression of the collective drives, conscious and unconscious, of American women, of their avowed obligations and their unconscious resistance. (1987: 168)

Having identified a link, Haskell assigns fixed meanings and reading positions, as if all female audiences use and understand the film text in exactly the same way. Nowhere does she address this issue in relation to how the institutional context influenced film form or its reception. Chapter two investigates the cultural studies intervention that identified the disregard for the socio-cultural context in which female spectators watched film. It turned away from the theoretical models defined by semiotics and psychoanalysis, denouncing them as essentialist, leaving little space for 'textual negotiation' (Gledhill 1988). Combining textual analyses with studies of audience reception and/or the economies of film culture, writers such as Christine Gledhill and Annette Kuhn identified a more complex and nuanced relationship between text, spectator and the institution of cinema. The cultural studies approach to film and the institution of cinema became less informed by an exclusive focus on the text than by ethnographic studies (Jackie Stacey and Jacqueline Bobo) or by a more interdisciplinary approach to contemporary culture (Tania Modleski and E. Ann Kaplan).

Another criticism of orthodox feminist film theory came from Black feminism regarding the failure to address race and ethnicity. What this revision proposed was that the Black woman functioned as the objectified Other within (white) feminist film theory. Jane Gaines in particular pointed to the elision of race in psychoanalytic models of sexual difference. Chapter three on race, ethnicity and post-colonialism explores the impact of postmodernity as well as post-colonial and subaltern theories on feminist film theory. Arguments offered by scholars such as Gaines, bell hooks (Gloria Watkins) and Lola Young spoke of historical silence and the cultural suppression of racial difference within film. These debates in turn contributed significantly to the understanding of hybridity and subject-identities related to the experience of post-colonialism and postmodernity as well as modified theories of female desire and subjectivities, and of female spectatorship.

Haskell's acknowledgement of unconscious drives anticipates later arguments by feminist theorists in the 1980s and 1990s about the role of fantasy and desire in the construction of visual pleasures as well as female subjectivity. Moving beyond the idea that male fantasy defines meaning, Haskell cautions the feminist critic from ignoring the fact that women's own 'rearguard fantasies of rape, sadism, submission, liberation and anonymous sex are as important a key to our emancipation, our self-understanding' (1987: 32). Chapter four investigates the interventions that speak about subjectivity, sexual difference and fantasy differently. In particular, it focuses on two phases: the 1980s and the revision of psychoanalytic theory; and the 1990s with the intervention from queer theory and lesbian/gay studies. Scholars rethought the limits of existing theories to develop ever more sophisticated readings of subjectivity, sexual difference and fantasy.

In much the same way as feminist film theory sought to deconstruct the workings of a film text from various perspectives by, in the words of Annette Kuhn, 'making visible the invisible' (1985: 73), the concluding chapter explores how feminist film studies functions as a discourse. In as much as feminist film theory aims to expose the ideological operations of patriarchy at work within textual and institutional practices, the field of feminist film studies is self-aware about the difficulties involved in articulating those arguments. Processes involved in discrediting, separating from, and even reclaiming and revising, past feminist debates reveal the perils involved in writing a feminist film theory.

Another thread that this book intends to pull out is how film feminism functions as a set of conceptual tools to articulate what can and cannot be said within dominant ideology. Speaking about such matters is to engage directly with structures of power and knowledge. Adapting a concept introduced by Tania Modleski, it is held that film feminism operates as a 'space of deferral' (1999: 22). By this is meant that feminist film theory operates to open up a critical space that allows women to enter into dialogue with each other and beyond the discipline. Not only does this talk seek to make sense of representation, subjectivity and experience but also confers new revelatory truths about these issues. Taking the discourse as a whole makes known the trials and tribulations involved in the process of writing theory. For it reveals the ambiguities involved when women speak within patriarchy as well as how film feminism as a field of knowledge gives representation for better or worse to the paradox.

Students from various humanities disciplines now routinely read feminist film theory. This book sets out to give students a sense of the different voices involved in producing that knowledge. It aims to root each debate within its intellectual context, to reveal how particular frameworks have shaped the approaches taken as well as explain the various goals, methodologies and interests guiding feminist film scholarship. Understanding origins and key concerns of what is being said will allow students to see how an academic argument is formed but also help them get a better sense of the research methods, intellectual ideas and critical perspectives used by film scholars to write new theories. Studying the body of work known as feminist film theory makes it possible to understand the contribution made by the discipline to producing new knowledge about gendered subjectivities, representation and spectatorship over the last four decades.

1 STRUCTURING A LANGUAGE OF THEORY

Claire Johnston begins her seminal article, 'Women's Cinema as Counter-Cinema' (2000a: 22–33) by taking issue with the sociological 'image of women' readings undertaken by the likes of Majorie Rosen and Molly Haskell. Her dismissal of a feminist film criticism that took as 'its starting point the manipulation of woman as sex objects' (1973: 3) heralded the emergence of new approaches to film theory and criticism shaped by the new continental theories of ideology, semiotics and subjectivity (especially the writings of Louis Althusser and Jacques Lacan). Her intervention indicated a significant theoretical shift from interpreting cinema as reflecting reality to understanding cinema as putting forward a particular ideological construction of reality. It led feminists to interrogate how the operations at work in the film text constituted meaning. Contemporary approaches to psychoanalysis opened out the discussion further and allowed feminist critics to contribute with new ideas about the unconscious processes involved in viewing a film. These various interventions into finding an appropriate language with which to articulate a theoretical position supplied new perspectives and a fresh direction for film feminism.

Before considering textual analysis as a crucial tool, and how this theoretical phase to structure a language for feminist film theory developed, it is important to recognise the intellectual context that made possible these groundbreaking theoretical interventions in the first place. Along with a number of women's film festivals – the New York International Festival of Women's Films (1972) and the Toronto

Women and Film Festival (1973) – and the publication of several books on feminist film criticism detailed in the introduction, film journals began to give space to the debate. Established film periodicals such as *Velvet Light Trap* devoted an entire issue to investigating the place of women within Hollywood in 1972. Newer film studies periodicals moved away from journalistic approaches and sociologically-based methodologies, to take up different theoretical positions and introduce new critical models in a bid to formulate a more 'scientific' theory of cinema. Especially after 1971, the British film journal *Screen* would extend the philosophical and methodological work initiated by post-1968 *Cahiers du cinéma* and become an important bridge in the migration of ideas from Europe to Britain and America. Training attention on linguistic/semiotics that explored ways of distinguishing film form from other cultural forms, and underpinned by a radical left-wing political agenda, the journal embarked on an ambitious project to theorise the relationship between 'ideological effects', cinema signification and subjectivity.[1] It first introduced the ideas of Althusser, Lacan and Christian Metz to Anglophone film theory, and pioneered the application of psychoanalysis (particularly the work of Sigmund Freud and Lacan) to the study of film and its visual pleasures. In particular it gave space to a feminist polemic searching for ways to explain how women are represented and positioned in cinema.

Among the first to be completely devoted to the feminist film theory debate was the West German journal *Frauen und Film*, founded by feminist filmmaker and critic Helke Sander in 1974. With its Marxist bias, the journal carried articles focused on denouncing women's cultural discrimination – her exclusion from producing dominant art forms, her image subject to sexist exploitation – as well as on formulating a feminist response aimed at identifying alternative cinematic codes and conventions for representing the woman on film. *Women and Film* (published in Berkeley, California between 1972–75) and later the feminist journal *m/f*, can be said to have initiated and developed further discussions on the politics of representation. Set up in 1976 by those previously working on *Women and Film*, *Camera Obscura: journal for feminism and film theory* illustrated the dynamics and urgency of the feminist engagement with film. Wanting to quickly move beyond the initial concerns – critiques of sexist ideologies and the recovery of a lost women's filmmaking history, the editors made known in the first issue their intention to offer a radical platform for the feminist film debate. The mission statement written by the editorial collective recognised that 'women are oppressed not only economically and politically but also in the very forms of reasoning, signifying and symbolical exchange of our culture' (*Camera Obscura* 1976: 3). The editors went further to propose that this oppression should be documented and analysed through textual analysis (to understand how meaning is produced by the film text) and the use of psychoanalysis (to make known the unconscious processes involved in constituting meaning). What these publications made possible was an intellectual space where feminist film analysis and criticism could take place.

Understanding the text

What distinguished British feminist film criticism from the sociological-based accounts was in part its emphasis on theory. Such an intervention was made possible by the adoption of theories and methods already being applied elsewhere within film studies to help unlock the specific operations that functioned within the film text to create meaning. Areas of existing film theory drawn upon by the feminist film critics at this time were informed by the advent of contemporary continental philosophies including semiotics (Saussurian structural linguistics/Barthesian semiotic theory) and poststructuralism (the structural-Marxist work of Althusser and post-1968 *Cahiers du cinéma* film criticism and genre theory). These theories not only made the feminist intervention possible by giving it a language with which to speak, but also legitimised the feminist theoretical position because of its standing within current academic thinking.

The appropriation of poststructuralism and semiotics meant that the primary focus of feminist inquiry was in the first instance on analysing the film text. Each methodological approach was predicated on an assumption that meaning, far from being imposed from the outside onto the film, was produced in and through the internal operations of the text itself. Neo-Marxist film criticism developed in *Screen*, for example, identified the 'classic realist text' as a model for understanding the ideology at work in Hollywood narrative cinema (MacCabe 1974). The classic realist/narrative text describes how bourgeois ideology is reproduced in the process of implicating the spectator within a representational world that is coherent and highly structured despite numerous voices vying for attention. Socio-cultural tensions remain hidden and are eventually eliminated as the dominant discourse overrules all other possible interpretations. Text-based criticism, shaped by pre-existing methodologies, demanded that critics make known how ideology produced knowledge about itself from within its own textual system.

To help feminists understand how to analyse the ideological operations at work in the text they turned to criticisms related to ideology, politics and cinema recently initiated by the influential French film journal, *Cahiers du cinéma*. Guided by recent developments in French poststructuralist thought, and intellectually shaped by the political events of May 1968, this newly developed politicised film criticism aimed to understand the text as a construct structured by ideology. The new theory identified the work of ideology as about seeking to conceal its own operations in the process of signifying meaning, as well as how those mechanisms could independently impact upon the production of meaning. Ideological analysis (as it was termed) emerged as a critical tool allowing critics to deconstruct the text: 'an ideological reading of a text is then a reconstruction of it in which what was previously hidden is now brought to light' (Kuhn 1985: 77).

Textual analysis aimed to break down the text into individual segments to allow for a reading of the underlying ideological operations at work in meaning production:

> Textual analysis … is founded on an understanding of texts as constructs, as structured by the work of ideology, while at the same time naturalising that work – embodying, in other words, denial or effacement of the operation of ideology. (Kuhn 1985: 84)

The usefulness of ideological analysis for feminist film theory is easy to see. Critics appropriating it could at least start to begin interrogating the repressive textual operations of patriarchal ideology that define woman as Other. Just as Roland Barthes (1973) noted that an effect of ideology is to make its signs appear part of the natural order, feminists pointed to how dominant filmmaking practices transmitted the ideological codes of patriarchy to construct an image of woman as somehow fixed. Poststructuralism and semiotics opened the way for feminists to conduct a more theoretically rigorous analysis of how a film's ideological operations constructed the idea of woman within its textual practices.

Feminist critics trained considerable attention on reading classical Hollywood films to uncover what dominant ideology concealed in the process of producing patriarchal knowledge. Their analyses place emphasis on the relationship between cinema, ideology and politics initiated by *Cahiers* editors Jean-Louis Comolli and Jean Narboni (1971). Originally published in 1970, their arguments were reprinted in *Screen* a year later in translation, coinciding with the first attempts made by feminists to think through the relations between ideology and the construction of woman as object. These writers argue that a system of ideology informs each film. Yet ideology does not always function in the same way within the text. To elaborate further, they devise a five-point inventory of how ideology operates in film, varying from films unequivocally endorsing dominant ideology to those openly subverting it. One category in particular piqued the interest of feminists; namely, those films that seem on the surface to adhere to the dominant ideology but, on further inspection, turn out to be far more complicated.[2] Those films appearing to open up and lay bare the operations of ideology intrigued feminists most. Taking their clue from *Cahiers* and their reading of *Young Mr Lincoln* (John Ford, 1939),[3] feminist textual analyses focused on ruptured texts to look for signs of ideological and formal contestation in relation to dominant film representations of women.

Feminists adopted *Cahiers* methods of ideological analysis – breaking the text down into smaller units, the detailed analysis of the hidden (unconscious) textual operations at work in each segment as well as across the whole film text – in its bid for legitimacy. The appropriation of (post)structuralist and semiological criticism reveals the need for feminist film theory to establish a coherent theoretical foundation on which to build a body of knowledge that could interrogate how the mechanisms of dominant ideology worked to produce particular representations of women. By aligning itself to such groundbreaking theoretical work, feminist film theory enhanced its credibility and strengthened its own critical authority to speak by invoking discourses (political philosophy, semiotics, psychoanalysis) whose intellectual importance went unquestioned.

Woman as textual sign

Claire Johnston (2000a) was one of the first feminist film critics to identify the film text as a semiotic sign system. Her intervention into existing male theoretical debates was, in the words of E. Ann Kaplan, a 'heady mix of Lacan, Althusser, Barthes and Foucault' (Kaplan 2000: 19). Indeed the density of ideas packed into her response articulates an urgency felt by feminists at this time to speak about how a sexist ideology positioned women in mainstream cinema.

Her investigation into the myth of woman in classical Hollywood films defines the woman as a structure in the film text. Indebted to Barthes' semiotic understanding of how myth works as a signifier of ideology,[4] she argues that myth invades film representation in much the same way as it does other cultural artefacts. She contends that, 'myth transmits and transforms that ideology of sexism and renders its invisible' (2000a: 24), stripping the sign 'woman' of its primary (denotative) meaning and substituting it with a symbolic (connotative) one. Hollywood cinema is governed by the same ideological operations in and through which the woman is constructed as a fixed sign:

> Iconography as a specific kind of sign or cluster of signs based on certain conventions within the Hollywood genres has been partly responsible for the stereotyping of women within the commercial cinema in general, but the fact that there is a far greater differentiation of men's roles than of women's roles in the history of the cinema relates to sexist ideology itself, and the basic opposition which places man inside history, and woman as ahistoric and eternal. (2000a: 23)

Adapting Barthesian semiotics allows Johnston to analyse the woman as a textual creation subject to the laws of verisimilitude (an impression of the real) involved in the making of film representation. Such a methodological approach helps her expose the unseen processes at work in how the affiliations of the classic realist text compel it to produce an image of the woman as myth, as a fixed signifier, responsible 'for the celebration of her non-existence' (2000a: 25).

Johnston applies her semiotic approach to discerning the internal operations of ideology in the classical Hollywood text, a semiotic sign system that represses or displaces the idea of woman. In spite of 'the enormous emphasis placed on women as spectacle in the cinema', she contends, 'woman as woman is largely absent' (ibid.). Yet by 'viewing the woman as sign within the sexist ideology', it is possible to see how the woman operates as a projection of male fantasies and fears. To clarify her point, she turns to films directed by Howard Hawks and John Ford, to examine the uneasy textual position of women. For example, woman operates as 'a traumatic presence that must be negated' (2000a: 27) in the Hawksian text. In the exclusive all-male universe, she endangers the coherence and future survival of the male group. While the woman is a source of anxiety that must somehow be disavowed within Hawks' signifying practices, she becomes an important if not ambivalent symbol of culture and home in Ford's. The female character emerges as a key convention in Ford films, essential to an internal tension revolving around the desire to roam and the desire to settle, the idea of the untamed wilderness and the idea of the cultivated garden. Embodying the idea of home, and with it the promise of domestication and culture, is the figure of the woman. Despite viewing Ford's textual system as potentially more progressive than Hawk's, she contends that the woman exists *only* as a sign that has meaning for men; in relation to herself she means nothing.

Even while acknowledging the inherent sexism in Hollywood's reliance on stereotypes, Johnston also notes that its products may display internal contradictions. Turning to Comolli and Narboni's typology, she advances the notion that studio films can function to critique dominant discourse if they produce enough internal contradictions. She modifies the internally self-critical text for feminist film theory into what she calls the '"progressive" classic film text' (2000b: 142):

> This internal criticism facilitates a process of de-naturalisation: behind the film's apparent coherence there exists an 'internal tension' so that the ideology no longer has an independent existence but is 'presented' by the film. The pressure of this tension cracks open the surface of the film; instead of its ideology being simply assumed and therefore virtually invisible, it is revealed and made explicit. (Ibid.)

Adapting Comolli and Narboni's category of films that internally break open to reveal the contradictory operations of dominant ideology at work permits her to describe the dislocations operating in the films of Dorothy Arzner, Nelly Kaplan and Ida Lupino. Why Johnston is particularly interested in Arzner is because she was virtually the only woman directing films during the heyday of the Hollywood studio system. Arzner's films are read by Johnston as working against the prevailing patriarchal culture through strategies of disruption and contradiction, 'between the discourses which the film text comprises and that of the ideology of patriarchal culture within which the film is placed' (ibid.). Put simply, Arzner's films are seen in some sense to rupture the ideological coherence of the classical Hollywood text.

'In general', Johnston continues, 'the woman in Arzner's films determines her own identity through transgression and desire in a search for an independent existence beyond and outside the discourse of the male' (ibid.). Internal textual tensions in her films are created between a classical Hollywood patriarchal narrative that never finds in favour of the woman and the 'discourse of the woman, or rather her attempt to locate it and make it heard' (ibid.). Johnston contends that juxtaposing male and female discourses gives Arzner's textual system its structural coherence. Privileging the female discourse as a structuring principle renders the male universe strange, disjointed and Other:

> In Arzner's films it is the universe of the male which invites scrutiny, which is rendered strange. In this way, the discourse of the male can no longer function as the dominant one ... It is only the discourse of the woman, and her desire for transgression, which provides the principle of coherence and generates knowledge, and it is in woman that Arzner locates the possibility of truth within the text. (2000b: 145)

For example, the discourse of woman in *Christopher Strong* (1933) cracks open the internal operations of dominant ideology to reveal contradiction, as Cynthia Darrington (Katharine Hepburn) transgresses patriarchal sexual-socio codes and conventions in her attempt to become a world champion aviatrix as well as find love with a married man. The ending – in which the unmarried heroine, pregnant by Strong, makes her bid for glory – reveals the central and un-resolvable narrative conflict between career and love. No longer able to tolerate the 'impossible contradictions' of her life, she removes her oxygen mask: she dies at the very moment she breaks the aviation record. 'Making strange' (borrowing from the Russian Formalist Shklovsky's use of the term '*ostranenie*') the very stereotypes Hollywood produces to call into question patriarchal ideology engages Arzner in 'a process of rewriting' (2000b: 148). Her work, whilst not considered by Johnston to create a radical new cinema, nonetheless 'opens up an area of contradiction in the text' (2000b: 147). By posing questions and offering a solution (of sorts) in the rewriting process, Arzner contributes to what Johnston sees as 'the development of a feminist counter-cinema' (2000b: 148).[5]

Pam Cook proposes similar strategies for thinking about how the self-critical text exposes the working of patriarchal ideology in the films of Arzner (1988: 46–56). She first urges the critic to understand film as a text requiring active reading. It is a position initiated by post-1968 *Cahiers* thinking on ideology as well as referenced by the popularity of Brechtian theories of spectator/text relations, otherwise known as 'distanciation' (or alienation effect), that circulated at the time. Identifying a specific system of representation produced by classical Hollywood cinema permits her to make a claim for how it locks the spectator into a fixed identificatory position (1988: 46). This closed relationship in turn prevents the spectator from experiencing contradiction or even questioning the dominant ideology. After establishing the spectators' position within the classical Hollywood textual system, she offers detailed analyses of how Arzner's films – *Merrily We Go To Hell* (1932) and *Dance, Girl, Dance* (1940) – seek to disrupt the fixed relationship between spectator and cinema. Cook proposes that Arzner's 'ironic methods' play with Hollywood's reliance on stereotypical images through making the scenes appear staged. Ironic distancing is created 'between image and narrative' (1988: 56) and function in a similar way to Brechtian 'distanciation' in the theatre. Cook's notion of what she calls the 'pregnant moment' shatters the illusionism of the image, to distance the spectator and disrupt identification. De-naturalising ideology in this way repositions the spectator. It allows them to critically engage with what is going on in the film as well as to interrogate their role as voyeur. Arzner's *oeuvre* emerges as much more politically subversive in Cook's work than in Johnston's.

Despite coming to different conclusions about how the internal textual ruptures function in the films of Dorothy Arzner, Cook and Johnston put forward a persuasive argument for suggesting how a feminist textual ideological analysis can help unlock even the most unpromising Hollywood text. These two theorists analyse the position of women in the films of Raoul Walsh, to suggest that woman 'is not only a sign in a system of exchange but an empty sign' (1990: 20). One exception is *The Revolt of Mamie Stover* (1956) where the film text centres on a self-reliant female protagonist played by Jane Russell. Here the heroine, while serving the same function as the male, operates differently: 'Her drive is not to test and transgress the Law as a means towards understanding a hidden secret within her past, but to transgress the forms of representation governing the classic cinema itself, which imprison her forever within an image' (1990: 22). Putting their newly developed feminist methodology to work gives them the tools not only to understand how narrative structures function to define Mamie's independence as rebellious but also to reveal how the text constitutes her as spectacle. They contend that the threat she poses to the patriarchal order (her success in business) is recuperated both at a narrative (she returns home with nothing after losing both her man and fortune at the end) and representational (Mamie/Russell is displayed as erotic object for visual contemplation) level: '[the] protagonist cannot write her own story: she is a signifier, an object of exchange in a play of desire between the absent subject and object of the discourse' (1990: 24). Nowhere is this sense that Mamie/Russell represents a spectacle of exchange more fully realised than in her role as performer and club hostess, her narrative downfall coinciding with her display as both an object of sexual and economic exchange. Such a position is made known through the continuous assertion of Mamie/Russell as image, as well as the male hero Jimmy (Richard Egan) who is 'constantly trying to write Mamie/Russell's story for her' (ibid.). All of which 'serves to repress the idea of female sexuality and to encase Mamie/Russell within the symbolic order, the Law of the Father' (1990: 25). Cook and Johnston's analysis make known the mechanisms involved in constituting Mamie/Russell as a constant source of textual tension, an unease caused by how her function as image works against her narrative position.

The work of Johnston and Cook in the early 1970s represents an ambitious attempt to establish the terms of a textual analysis from a feminist perspective as well as describe the role of the feminist critic in the process. Janet Bergstrom sums up the usefulness of this feminist intervention in her 1979 review:

> An insistence on a theoretical rather than a sociological approach to feminist filmmaking and criticism, a recognition of the importance of feminist criticism and theory *for* feminist filmmaking, an emphasis on the importance of an understanding of how the representation of women operates in classical narrative film ... the introduction of topics within feminist theory such as woman-as-sign, the relationship between woman, representation and fetishism. (1979: 25)

Such an approach recognises how the internal operations of a cinematic textual system renders woman as sign under patriarchy and, in so doing, represses the feminine through constituting the woman as absent. Whether examining the films of the proto-feminist Dorothy Arzner or the patriarchal Raoul Walsh, feminist textual analysis appropriated for feminism the theories and methodologies of poststructuralism and semiotics as well as ideological analysis. Such readings involve a reconstruction of the film text in which what was previously hidden is now made known in and through the act of textual analysis. The place of the critic as interpreter, to make known meaning, is crucial.

Psychoanalysis and film theory

Undertaking close textual analysis is predicated on the assumption that meaning is not always easily discernible. Detailed textual readings are carried out to uncover the processes involved not only in the production of textual meaning but also in the relationship between text and spectator. Inseparable from the importance of semiotic and ideological analyses to answering these questions is the influence of psychoanalysis. Psychoanalytic theories are used in the work of Johnston and Cook, but also employed more rigorously by theorists such as Laura Mulvey, to develop new theories about identification, visual pleasure and the (male) gaze as well as female subjectivity and desire. If poststructuralism and semiotics focus on how the text produces woman as Other, then psychoanalytic-based theories proceed to describe the psychic processes involved in constituting that meaning within spectating practices.

Appropriating psychoanalytic discourse for feminist film theory derived from a dialogue between psychoanalysis and cinema already taking place elsewhere within film studies. It was a debate that asked, in the words of Christian Metz, 'how can [psychoanalysis] contribute to the study of the cinema signifier?' (1983: 21). Psychoanalytic theory shifted from a semiotic concern with the text, to consider instead the unconscious processes involved in how the spectator is positioned in and through the film text. It posed the question of, as Annette Kuhn writes, 'how ... in the moment of reading, spectators are caught up in, and formed by, and at the same time construct, meanings' (1985: 44). Key to this intervention was the absorption of ideas from a number of psychoanalytic thinkers, most notably Freud and the post-Freudian psychoanalyst Lacan. What distinguished the psychoanalytic approach was that it rested on theories of subject formation that could begin to understand the position of a viewing subject that is at once constituted by and constituting cinema.

'Cinema', Metz contends, 'involves us in the imaginary' (1983: 45).[6] Nowhere is the artificial state of regression so effectively initiated than in the darkened auditorium where the inactive spectator-subject becomes captivated by moving images. With Lacanian thought central to his theoretical intervention, he argues that the cinema screen operates as another type of mirror taking us back to the Imaginary (a founding moment in which the origins of subjectivity are formed in the image). The immobility of the film viewing experience lifts psychic controls and lulls the spectator into an infantile state where fantasy remains unchecked. Invoking the mirror analogy allows him to identify the cinema screen as another site where the subject takes pleasure in the imaginary completeness of a projected image. What happens on screen implicates the spectator in a unique play of imaginary presence (perceptual experiences – fantasies, dreams, illusions) and real absence (what is represented but not really there) similar to the illusionary (pleasurable) unity experienced by the child in the mirror phase. Reaching similar conclusions is Jean-Louis Baudry (1986a; 1986b). Grounding his theory in a Freudian analysis of dream-images and 'dream-work' enables him to explore the impact of cinema technology on the psyche of the spectator, and how an impression of the real is constituted. He contends that a mode of subjectivity equivalent to the dream-state is instituted in and through the cinema apparatus: 'The cinematographic projection is reminiscent of dream' (1986b: 308).

Metz goes further in his discussion of identification and the spectator to notice an important difference with Lacan's mirror phase. Contrary to the child who perceives itself in the image, the spectator's own image is not represented on screen: 'the reflection of the own body has disappeared' (1983: 46). He explains why:

> What makes possible the spectator's absence from the screen – or rather the intelligible unfolding of the film despite that absence – is the fact that the spectators already know the experience of the mirror (of the true mirror). (Ibid.)

Instead the spectator identifies not with their image but with themselves 'as a pure act of perception' (1983: 49) – an act made possible because the subject has *already* moved through the Imaginary into the realm of the Symbolic,[7] and thus completed and understood the experience of splitting in the mirror phase: 'The imaginary of the cinema presupposes the symbolic, for the spectator must first of all have known the primordial mirror' (1983: 57). Watching a film entails that the spectator recognises the other on screen; and 'as for me, I am there to look at him. I take no part in the perceived, on the contrary, I am *all-perceiving*' (1983: 48). His response to this omnipotent seeing position is to argue that the spectator gains 'perceptual mastery' in identifying with the apparatus that sees all – the camera and its substitute within the cinema, the film projector:

> The film is what I receive, and it is also what I release, since it does not pre-exist my entering the auditorium and I only need to close my eyes to suppress it. Releasing it, I am the projector, receiving it, I am the screen; in both these figures together, I am the camera, which points and yet which records. (1983: 51)

'The passion for seeing' (1983: 52), reactivating archaic pleasures linked to the Imaginary, occurs when the spectator believes themselves part, and 'duplicating' the work of, the optical machines that see all.

Another contribution made by Metz to film theory explains how psychoanalytic concepts that relate the desire to look with sexual (libidinal) drives could help us understand the unconscious processes at work in the viewing experience. Grounded in Freud's theories of the look – 'the desire to see (=scopic drive, scopophilia, voyeurism)' (1983: 58),[8] his work is concerned with how scopophilia (looking as a source of pleasure), determined in and through the machinery of cinema, relies on fetishism and disavowal ('I know but...'). Freud suggests that scopophilia depends, for the subject to experience pleasure, on a gap between subject and object as well as on a futile pursuit to recover an object that is permanently lost. Desire is activated in this play of distance and absence. Presenting an object for the spectator to look at as both distant and absent makes film especially inclined to arouse libidinal energy that overrides conscious awareness.

Another film theorist using psychoanalytic theory in the early 1970s was Raymond Bellour. Concentrating on individual films, especially those made by Alfred Hitchcock, he reveals the Oedipal fantasies and desire at work within a film text linked to socio-cultural formations of sexuality and sexual difference (1972; 1977). He demonstrates how sexual difference serves to structure the text/spectator relationship. His analyses of Hitchcock's *The Birds* (1963) makes known, for example, how the text and its address find in favour of the male spectator. A shot-by-shot analysis of Melanie Daniels' (played by Tippi Hedren) return boat trip across Bodega Bay to deliver a pair of lovebirds to Mitch Brenner (Rod Taylor), and her attack by a seagull, illustrates his argument. Looking at alternation, repetition and variation within the arrangement of the shots leads him to conclude that the woman, both as image and in the way she returns the look, is predicated on lack. Woman is image or subjugated within the narrative (either she is disciplined or subject to domination by a man). Either way she compensates the male spectator for his own anxieties about lack through a fantasy of woman that bolsters his illusion of authority and completeness.

Implicit in the work of Metz and Baudry, but made explicit in Bellour, is the idea that the cinema spectator is male. Indeed, the notion of the male Oedipal subject is an assumption that pervades the very structures of the psychoanalysis discourse, and is symptomatic of the difficulties Freud had in theorising the construction of female subjectivity (see chapter four). Lacan's return to Freud revises the Oedipal struggle, shifting the site of conflict from nature (anatomical development) to nurture (cultural signification). While persistently maintaining that the penis is *not* the phallus (the phallus is a signifier), and identifying that the phallus (the signifier of lack) eludes *both* sexes to reveal the precariousness of sexual identity, his account still privileges the masculine in this seemingly fixed structure. From Bellour's Oedipal fantasies and Baudry's daydreaming spectator to Metz's voyeur identifying with the work of the cinematic apparatus, film theory at this point constructs the cinema spectator as male while the object of that gaze is female.

Moreover, the position of the male theorist/critic in revealing how the text makes visible unconscious desire adds another dimension. Introducing a complexity and variety of ideas on the unconscious and psychical processes involved in spectating, ones that would fascinate feminists over the years, these theorists put forward a series of psychoanalytic-based statements by which desire and spectatorship could be known. Metz was in fact well aware of his own desire to locate the absent cinematic object and turn it into an object of knowledge, and he called on others to do the same. Bellour responded to Metz's challenge to study his own Imaginary, to position himself in relation to the film text in the process of knowing it.

Within this double movement of masculine spectatorship/readership, how might the woman achieve subjectivity, or the female viewing subject take pleasure in the image from within a phallocentric system that excludes her? In articulating these questions, feminist film theorists took cinema apparatus theorists like Metz to task for their elision of sexual difference (Rose 1988: 200–6) and articulated a problem in the process.

Crucial to the feminist study of psychoanalysis in cinema is a belief that scopophilic drives (fetishism and structures of disavowal), Oedipal narratives that find in favour of the male, the attraction to cinematic images based on archaic pleasures linked to the Imaginary are predicated on the concept of woman. 'An idea of woman stands as lynch pin to the system' advocates Laura Mulvey: '[It] is her lack that produces the phallus as a symbolic presence, it is her desire to make good the lack that the phallus signifies' (1975: 6). Feminist scholarship thus identified a gap in the contributions cited above. They noted that male psychoanalytic theory failed to grasp the importance of woman within the Symbolic; her significance seemingly at an end once her lack precipitates crisis and the child moves away from her (and the pre-Oedipal stage/Imaginary) into the world of language and the Law of the Father. After this time, she remains nothing but a memory, 'which oscillates between memory of maternal plenitude and memory of lack' (1975: 6–7). For feminists, woman represented more than 'castration and nothing else' (1975: 6).

Broadly speaking, the appropriation of psychoanalysis into feminist film theory had two phases, each emphasising Lacan and/or the ideas developed by Freud in his later work on sexuality and sexual difference. The first dealt with the question of spectator/text relations within the apparatus of dominant cinema (or classical Hollywood cinema). It aimed at challenging psychoanalytic orthodoxy on pleasurable looking as well as the status of the woman-as-image within narrative. The second intervention focused on understanding desire and the concept of fantasy (explored further in chapter four). Contesting the conventional wisdom about the subjugation of woman's desire to offer, as Mulvey put it, 'her image as bearer of the bleeding wound' (1975: 7), feminist scholarship broadened the debate. Feminist interventions bringing together psychoanalysis with feminism provided critical tools to open out the text for feminist readings in particular while rethinking psychoanalytic terminology – disavowal, fetishism, identification and the Imaginary – for film theory in general.

Visual pleasures and questions of spectatorship

No other single article in the feminist film theory canon has impacted so widely as Mulvey's seminal essay 'Visual Pleasure and Narrative Cinema'. Originally published in *Screen* in 1975, it represented both a dialogue with and radical challenge to discussions already taking place within film studies and beyond – Juliet Mitchell's 1974 'return to Freud' thesis entitled *Psychoanalysis and Feminism* is one example. Mulvey's study marked a polemical response against existing accounts of the woman-as-image and how the look operated in classic realist/narrative Hollywood texts, to indicate, as Vicky Lebeau summarises, 'a moment of anxiety and desire for *something else* in feminist film theory and practice' (2001: 95). Framed by the Athusserian/Lacanian approach to cinema signification adopted by *Screen*, and drawing on psychoanalytic (combining Freud with Lacan) and existing feminist theories, Mulvey moved the debate on spectatorship further than other critics working in this area at the time – including Metz and Bellour – by taking the discussion off into an entirely new and feminist direction.

Mulvey turns to psychoanalytic studies on the scopophilic subject – most notably Freud's child who desires to control the object through the gaze and Lacan's jubilant infant caught in the image – as 'a political weapon' to psychoanalyse 'the way the unconscious of patriarchal society has structured film form' (1975: 6). She begins with the contention that dominant cinema, as exemplified by Hollywood, appeals to a preconscious desire for pleasurable looking. Deconstructing how the subject gains pleasure in looking would, she argues, reveal the manner in which the patriarchal unconscious genderises those pleasures: 'Unchallenged, mainstream film coded the erotic into the language of the dominant patriarchal order' (1975: 8). Patriarchy encodes a gender imbalance within ways of seeing, in which 'the pleasure in looking has been split between active/male and passive/female' (1975: 11).

Chief among the pleasures offered is that of voyeuristic-scopophilic gazing, where the spectator gains gratification from indulging in unlicensed looking at an image, typically of a woman. The active and curious (male) gaze translates the (female) image into an object of sexual fantasy, so granting the voyeur a position defined by control and mastery with its implied separation from the source of erotic stimulation. Narcissistic (mis)recognition of self in an idealised figure on screen, typically the male hero, is the other visual pleasure; a structure of seeing that allows for a 'temporary loss of ego while simultaneously reinforcing it' (1975: 10). Replicating the child's discovery of its own image during the Lacanian mirror scenario, the spectator 'projects his look onto that of his like, his screen surrogate, so that the power of the male protagonist as he controls events coincides with the active power of the erotic look, both giving a satisfying sense of omnipotence' (1975: 12). Structured in the language of the patriarchal unconscious (instinctual libidinal drives and processes of ego formation), visual pleasures in dominant cinema constitute the spectator as male while the woman 'holds the look, and plays to and signifies male desire' (1975: 11). In turn, this gendered active/passive divide structures film narrative with the male hero advancing the story and the woman-as-image disrupting narrative movement, 'to freeze the flow of action in moments of erotic contemplation' (ibid.).

The sight of woman stimulates pleasure, her 'appearance coded for strong visual and erotic impact ... [connotes a] *to-be-looked-at-ness*' (ibid.). Yet, and at the same time, her image provokes anxiety for the spectator. Because she constitutes the castrated male Other, a signifier of sexual difference, the woman as object is concomitant with the threat of castration that needs to be somehow disavowed. To allay castration fears the film narrative renders the woman-as-image non-threatening through two basic strategies. The first associates voyeurism with sadism: 'pleasure lies in ascertaining guilt (immediately associated with castration), assert-ing control and subjugating the guilty person' (1975: 14). The narrative here is concerned with investigating the 'woman' in order to demystify and control her, resulting finally in her punishment, devaluation or moral rescue. She is subjected to and subordinated by the male gaze as he tries to gain control and discipline her for arousing forbidden desire in him. An undercover investigation in *Vertigo* (Alfred Hitchcock, 1958) gives Scottie Fergusson (James Stewart) license to scrutinise the spectacle of Madeleine (Kim Novak), 'a perfect image of female beauty and mystery' (1975: 16). Soon sexual attraction turns into an obsession with mastering her image, as he sadistically forces Judy to become 'Madeleine'. The film concludes with Scottie exposing Judy's guilt and her death: 'True perversion is barely concealed under a shallow mask of ideological correctness – the man is on the right side of the law, the woman on the wrong' (1975: 15).

The second strategy is fetishism. Drawing on its original significance within Freudian accounts of sexual difference (Freud 1977a), Mulvey demonstrates how turning the woman-as-image (as opposed to the cinematic apparatus identified by Metz) into fetish conceals castration anxiety. Rather than lacking, the woman-as-image is idealised as being complete. The flawless female body, or parts of it at least, are given an importance to compensate for the lack that she originally signified, hence the excessive over-valuation of the female star-image – Greta Garbo's face, Marilyn Monroe's mouth, Marlene Dietrich's legs. Translating the woman into fetish diverts attention away from the female 'lack' – her lack of penis, her bleeding wound – so that she no longer represents a menacing figure but an idealised spectacle of beauty and perfection. 'She is no longer the bearer of guilt but a perfect product, whose body, stylised and fragmented by close-ups, is the content of the film and the direct recipient of the spectator's look' (1975: 14).

Voyeuristic-scopophilic looking (pleasure in subjecting another person in the gaze) and identificatory processes (constitution of the ego) are crucial in constituting visual pleasures, argues Mulvey. Such pleasures are dependent on 'three different looks' in the cinema, 'that of the camera as it records the pro-filmic event, that of the audience as it watches the final product, and that of the characters at each other within the screen illusion' (1975: 17). Convention demands that narrative films deny the presence of the camera and initiate distance between the spectator and screen. In turn, these two looks must be disavowed for a believable on-screen world to be created in which the male hero operates. It is, however, the woman-as-image evoking castration anxiety that threatens to disrupt the circuit of inter-connected looks and male desire, and expose the fiction as illusion. She concludes by advocating for a new feminist aesthetic. One that destroys the conventional relay of looks involved in producing visual pleasures, 'to free the look of the camera into its materiality in time and space and the look of the audience into dialectics and passionate detachment' (1975: 18).

It is imperative to place the 'Visual Pleasure' thesis within its historical and intellectual context to understand its founding moment status:

Out of the Women's Liberation Workshop in which consciousness-raising, political practice and intellectual innovation were all valued and, for a time, kept in balance. Secondly ... the 'high theory' strand of British theory was influenced by the intellectual climate created by the New Left Review's break with the specific

English-ness of British left culture and politics. We looked to France for our theory and to Hollywood cinema for critical raw material. In the 1960s, the *New Left Review* had translated Althusser and Lacan, both of whom were to influence feminist film theory, into English for the first time. (Mulvey 1989: 68–9)

Mulvey's essay represented an enormous theoretical leap forward for feminist film theory in particular and film studies in general: 'a jump from the ungendered and formalistic analyses of semiotics to the understanding that film viewing always involves gendered identities' (Humm 1997: 17). It identified the spectator as constituted within a set of psychical relations, interpellated by film language (edits, narrative) and apparatus (the camera). She makes explicit the gender implications of psychoanalytic-inspired film theory that involve voyeurism, narcissistic identification and fetishism as well as how the woman-as-image inspires castration anxiety predicated on the Oedipal trajectory when the male child first encounters sexual difference. Simultaneous denial and suppression of the feminine is quite literally played out in how the narrative and look of the camera position the female figure either as a fetishistic idealisation or subject of voyeuristic punishment. Her work helps us understand how dominant cinema constitutes the spectator as male and the phallocentrism of desire, in which male subjectivity is the *only* subject position made available. '[P]sychoanalysis can be used', Mulvey would later write, 'to reveal the way in which conventions of narrative cinema are tailored to dominant masculine desires ... it is organised around male erotic privilege' (1979: 9). Seeing no escape from these patriarchal structures of looking prompts her to call for the destruction of visual pleasures, both in relation to feminist film aesthetics and as a critical strategy.

Case study: Rear Window and visual pleasures

Alfred Hitchcock's 1954 suspenseful thriller finds L. B. Jeffries (James Stewart) witnessing a murder committed in the building across from his own. Confined to his room and incapacitated because of broken leg means photo-journalist Jeffries is bound to his seat in much the same way as the spectator. 'Hitchcock's skilful use of identification processes and liberal use of subjectivity camera from the point of view of the male protagonist draw the spectators deeply into his position, making them share his uneasy gaze' (Mulvey 1975: 16). Looking is central to the *Rear Window* text, 'oscillating between voyeurism and fetishistic fascination' (ibid.).

The gaze takes on an erotic dimension when trained on his girlfriend, Lisa (Grace Kelly). Constructed as an image of 'visual perfection' through her narrative status as a model obsessed with fashion and feminine style means she is presented as an object of sexual fantasy for the spectator. Frustrated with Jeffries' obsession with events across the court she pulls down the window blinds to direct his gaze away from the neighbours onto her. Lisa quite literally halts the narrative investigation to present herself as erotic spectacle for Jeffries. Yet as Mulvey points out he has little interest in her until she crosses over from his room to the Thorwald apartment. Jeffries watches her 'as a guilty intruder exposed by a dangerous man threatening her with punishment' (1975: 17) through his camera lens but his immobile state means he is unable to save Lisa from the clutches Lars Thorwald (Raymond Burr). By means of identification with Jeffries, through aligning with his gaze, the spectator is complicit with his masochistic visual pleasures.

Review: woman as absent

Reviewing a decade of debate and radical filmmaking in 1979, Laura Mulvey assesses the initial contribution made by second-wave feminism to film criticism.

> It was ... feminism that gave a new urgency to the politics of culture, exemplified the contradictions inherent in a desire to build a counter-culture, and focused on connections between oppression and command of language. (1979: 3)

What defined the first encounter between film theory and feminism was a common interest in the politics of representation and the way in which dominant cinema produced textual meaning and constituted its spectator. Cracking open these closed and homogenous textual systems and structures of cinematic identification to reveal how the sign of woman is repressed within the unconscious structures of patriarchy defined the work of these feminist theorists. In turn, the feminist project was indelibly marked by the new continental theories of the text (Barthes), ideology (Althusser) and subjectivity (Lacan) that demonstrated how dominant discourse worked to obscure underlying political and material aims. Early feminist film theory can be said to have initiated a field of study that revealed how patriarchal discourse knows gender as well as the ways in which 'the image of woman in patriarchal representation refers more readily to its connotations within the male unconscious' (1975: 8).

Mulvey saw the aim of a feminist film theory to break with patriarchal pleasures and 'to conceive a new language of desire' (ibid.). The next step would be for the discourse to move beyond a position where the woman is defined as Other to one where resistance, difference and change can be conceived. Yet the problem facing feminists was how to construct a theory from a language ordered by patriarchal signification. Appropriating Lacanian theory may allow feminists to identify how the subject is constituted in and as an effect of language, but his account of subjectivity (the self is constituted in language acquisition) excludes woman; in fact, as he insists, the woman cannot exist.[9] She is not only what the male is not (bearer of lack, the 'not-all') but embodies the site of desire – *jouissance* (pleasure experienced as euphoric and orgasmic bliss beyond the Symbolic).

Working with and in closed patriarchal structures soon presented feminist scholarship with a paradox; namely, that access to pleasure and desire for the female spectator is *only* made possible through masculine identification. Mulvey was to return to the masculinisation of the female gaze; drawing on Freud's theory of femininity, she claims that Hollywood narrative cinema regresses the female spectator to a pre-Oedipal developmental stage; it is moment of action, which is later repressed as the girl adopts femininity. 'Trans-sexual identification' defines the uneasy position assigned to the female spectator; it involves an internal oscillation between feminine passivity and a regressive but active masculine position that allows the female spectator to engage with the narrative. This transvestism is constituted in the structures of male looking and identificatory patterns. Mulvey's work on gendered looking and pleasure in cinema paved the way in feminist film theory for the development of analyses and conceptual models that would address the thorny question of the female spectator.

Dilemmas over defining the female spectator and explaining feminine visual pleasures structured by (masculine) voyeurism and fetishism are questions that absorbed others. E. Ann Kaplan, writing about women in Hollywood cinema, analyses that while the female can possess the gaze and even look at the male character, she cannot desire within such a phallocentric textual system. The gaze is not necessarily male, 'but to own and activate the gaze, given our language and the structures of the unconscious, is to be in the "masculine" position' (1983: 10). Teresa de Lauretis is no more hopeful than Kaplan or Mulvey when speaking about the desiring female spectator. Offering a semiotic understanding of the structural representation of women in cinema, and understanding the logic of dominant narrative as a classic masculine Oedipal trajectory, de Lauretis acknowledges how textual narrative divides spectatorship along gender lines:

> to say that narrative is the production of Oedipus is to say that each reader – male or female – is constrained and defined within the two positions of a sexual difference thus conceived: male-hero-human, on the side of the subject; the female-obstacle-boundary-space, on the other. (1984: 121)

Developing her argument further she distinguishes two distinct identificatory processes in operation. The first involves an oscillating either/or identification, between an active (masculine) identification with the gaze, and a passive (feminine) identification with the image. The second process consists of a both/and identification, meaning a double identification shifting between the figure of narrative movement and the figure of narrative image. Such simultaneous figural identification makes it possible for the female spectator to adopt both the active and passive positions in relation to desire: 'Desire for the other, and desire to be desired by the other' (1984: 143). Yet, while double identification may produce surplus pleasure, it is also the very mechanism by which a cinematic narrative both reflects and sustains social forms of oppression against women. It leads de Lauretis to claim that the notion of woman in cinema – as subject in the text, or spectator finding pleasure in the narrative – is a possible contradiction in terms, to such an extent that the female subject is a 'non-subject' (1984: 36).

Feminist film theory is grounded in the paradox of the unrepresentability of the feminine. While Lacanian psychoanalytic thinking provides radical ideas on the complex formation of both subject and object through discourse, doubts persist about biological determinism and phallocentrism (Gallop 1981: 247). Psychoanalysis' uncompromising insistence on how sexual identity requires each individual to take up a fixed position in relation to the phallus was felt by many to be reductive and lead to essentialism. Furthermore, analyses produced by the likes of Mulvey, Johnston and Cook hinged on a similar deterministic logic that mapped unconscious processes involved in constituting gender identities on to structures of looking and meaning production in dominant cinema. Such closed systems made it almost impossible to find spaces for resistance and difference while revealing 'the *difficulty* of femininity as a sexual position or category in relation to the symbolic' (Penley 1985: 52). It is a predicament Mulvey later recognised: 'Psychoanalytic theory offered something besides an appropriate critical vocabulary and an analytic tool; it offered a new and different kind of pleasure that compensated, in a way, for the sense of loss' (1989: 249). Feminist appropriation of psychoanalysis and semiotics contributed immeasurably to the critical armoury of feminist film theory to advance understanding of meaning production and visual pleasures. However, in the process of structuring a language, the woman – as subject on screen, reader of film texts, consumer of cinema – appeared in danger of vanishing from view.

2   TEXTUAL NEGOTIATIONS: FEMALE SPECTATORSHIP
           AND CULTURAL STUDIES

Christine Gledhill contends that theories of woman as a textual sign were too abstract and did not go far enough in addressing cultural issues. '[Femininity] is not simply an abstract textual position; and what women's history tells us about femininity lived as a socio-culturally, as well as a psychically differentiated category, must have consequences for our understanding of the formation of feminine subjectivity, of the feminine textual spectator and the viewing/reading of female audiences' (1988: 67). Such an assessment challenges the ahistoricism of feminist thinking shaped by semiotics and psychoanalysis as well as the use of a monolithic concept of ideology defined as patriarchal and predicated upon rigid binary oppositions. Too much attention, Gledhill argued, had been given over to the primacy of the film text; and to studying it in isolation to understand how the internal textual mechanisms produce meaning and constitute the spectator. Those who shared Gledhill's concerns agreed that text-based criticism offered little scope for dealing with questions related to the specific cultural and socio-historical context in which films were produced and consumed as well as to institutional issues related to production, distribution and exhibition strategies. Questions raised by these feminist scholars concerning what they saw as 'the gulf between textual analysis and contextual inquiry' (Kuhn 1992: 304) provided a space for interrogating anew the relationship between the text, the institutional and socio-cultural context, and the female spectator/reader.

    Stemming in part from a response to Laura Mulvey's thesis on visual pleasures and the phallocentric male gaze, feminists working in the field of cultural studies moved the debate on from an understanding of the textual spectator (someone constituted in the film text) to 'a consideration of the continuity between women's interpellation as spectators and their status as a social audience' (Kuhn 1992: 310). Soon revealed in this investigation into cinematic identification and socio-cultural readership was a gap between feminism and real women, between political ideology and personal experience, between how feminist theory interpreted texts and how actual women audiences made use of them. Work focused mainly on neglected material drawn from popular culture and the mass media, and led to the discovery of generic products – such as melodrama and soap opera – designed primarily for female audiences. What these lines of inquiry made known was that spectating positions were much more complex than previously suggested. Framing this debate I turn first to the emergence of cultural studies as an academic discipline which would make it possible to think differently about the relationship between feminist film theory, media texts and the female spectator with the introduction of different methodologies and research protocols.

Cultural studies

Attempts made by feminist scholars to theorise female spectatorship anew were made possible through a wider engagement with the burgeoning field of British cultural studies in the 1970s. With the establishment of the Centre for Contemporary Cultural Studies at the University of Birmingham in 1964, feminist thinking came to be shaped by theoretical approaches and methodologies adopted by the department. Rooted in a post-Marxist concern with the subversive capabilities of cultural practices and mass culture, cultural studies-inspired scholarship was committed to understanding popular culture and questions of consumption. Textual analysis combined with an acute awareness of the specific historical and socio-cultural context defined this inter-disciplinary methodology. Similar to early feminist film theory, it grew out of poststructuralist approaches to theorising ideology (Althusserian Marxism, Lacanian psychoanalysis, Barthes and semiotics, Lévi-Strauss and myth).[1] Combining theory with the political, it found new ways of thinking about how ideology produced meaning in, and constituted individuals as subjects within, cultural institutions, texts and practices. The bi-annual papers published by the Centre from 1972 to 1977, entitled *Working Papers in Cultural Studies*, as well as the newly-founded but short-lived journal *Ideology and Consciousness* (1977–80) created space for these debates to flourish.

Scholars like Stuart Hall (1980) and David Morley (1980b) took 1970s *Screen* film theory to task for analysing the text/reader encounter without reference to social and historical context. With the textual spectator of semiotic-psychoanalytic film theory rejected, cultural studies concentrated on the empirical audience predicated on a long-standing interest in underrepresented groups (based on class, age, gender and ethnicity) and debates on cultural consumption. Pratibha Parmar speaks about her involvement, as a postgraduate student at the Centre, in writing *The Empire Strikes Back: Race and Racism in 70s Britain*: 'Our project was to examine the everyday lived experiences of black British people as culture' (2000: 379). This publication introduced new critical paradigms for understanding race, Black culture and race relations, to offer an 'alternative discourse around issues of race, gender, national identity, sexual identity, and culture [that] marked a turning point' (2000: 280). It also reveals how the cultural studies intervention into feminist film theory contributed new methodologies and approaches to research, including empirical and ethnographic studies. Alternative subjectivities were proposed from these findings based on class, gender identity, sexual orientation, regional identity, race and ethnicity, and personal experience. It further identified never before discussed generic material as well as complex viewing positions related to identities beyond the white, middle-class heterosexual norm.

Central to the work carried out here was an attempt to devise a model that explains how the communicative process operates within a specific cultural context. Hall's 'preferred reading' theory (1980), originally devised in 1973, proposed an encoding/decoding model. Amalgamating different approaches to analysing the media audience, and assimilating sociological and cultural theories (rooted in Antonio Gramsci's theory of hegemony),[2] this model identifies a polysemic cultural text able to elicit different responses from its audience. This on-going struggle over meaning involves how meanings are 'encoded' by producers, how dominant ideology structures 'preferred' meanings in the text, and how readers/spectators 'decode'. Audience decipherment represents another site of contestation involving acceptance, negotiation or opposition. Dependent on where the individual is positioned within the social structure, and how they are shaped by affiliations associated with class, gender, sexuality and/or ethnicity, reader/spectator response is determined either by aligning with, negotiating or even opposing the 'preferred' meanings at the moment of reception. What this means is that while audiences draw on roughly similar discourses when decoding a text, and that those available readings are ultimately restricted by the text, how the individual makes sense of it can never be totally determined by the text's 'preferred' meanings.

Developing Hall's claims about how the spectator negotiates meaning, Morley (1980b) contributed with a shift in emphasis towards understanding the empirical audience. Undertaking an ethnographic study of audience responses to the British early evening news programme, *Nationwide*, led him to conclude that the interaction between text and reader is far more complex than the textual spectator model would have us believe. Negotiating meaning is dependent upon a discursive reading context. What his research found was that viewers are actively engaged in making meaning but these acts of reading fail to conform in any clear-cut socio-economic positionings.

Growing feminist interest in such approaches to text-reader relationships allowed feminist scholars to move beyond the textual determinism of the semiotic and psychoanalytic accounts to survey a more complex range of responses made by actual women to the film/television text. Challenging the alleged passivity identified by the textual model of spectatorship was particularly important for these academics exploring questions of women as cultural consumers. With women given an assumed passive position within patriarchal culture as well as in the semiotic-psychoanalytic model of spectatorship, and women audiences associated with the most derived cultural forms (soap operas, women's weepie, romance fiction), feminist academics came to challenge this culturally ascribed position of negativity. Investigating ways in which women actively negotiate media texts allowed them to set out much more discursive reading processes than previously suggested (Kuhn 1985; Gledhill 1988; Modleski 1994). Such a discussion of female pleasures and reading positions grew out of a necessity in the context where 'the personal *is* political'. It was research that would, in the words of Sarah Franklin, Celia Lury and Jackie Stacey, 'engage with the "personal" dimensions of culture in the political context of a feminist analysis' (1991: 6).

Cultural studies, popular pleasures and television audiences

The 1980s saw an increased interest in audience research and reception studies. Whereas feminist film criticism at this time focused on the spectator as constituted in the film text, cultural studies feminists were far more interested in the empirical audience. Much of this ethnographic work trained attention on television (rather than film) viewing pleasures and consumption – and more recently videos watched at home (Walkerdine 1986; Gray 1992). In contrast to film theory, in which the text was privileged over context, those working in television studies favoured understanding the context in which the text was produced and consumed.

Central to this work was the question about the specific forms of pleasures which female audiences find appealing. But conclusions proved unsettling for feminist scholarship. Tania Modleski (1994; 1999) and Janice Radway (1987), in their respective works on female readership and the enduring popularity of romantic fiction within a post-feminist age, interrogate what it is about these tales of naïve heroines swept away by dashing heroes that continues to attract an eager female fan base. Modleski in particular notes that, while popular cultural forms are routinely dismissed as derivative and worthless, they offer potent fantasies for a voracious female readership ready 'to participate in and actively desire feminine self-betrayal' (1994: 37) for complex and often contradictory reasons. Radway contributes further with her observation that the consumption of romantic literature acts to mediate female experience and expectations. While second-wave feminism told women that popular cultural forms for women (Harlequin Romance, fashion, the 'woman's film', daytime soap operas) were politically bad for them, female readers/spectators continue to find genuine pleasure in cultural forms that put women back into their traditional place. Feminist scholarship finds no straightforward answers to the paradox but remains convinced that answers must be somehow found.

One of the first scholars to contribute to the debate on television viewing habits, popular pleasures and the female spectator was Dorothy Hobson (1982). Her ethnographic research focuses on the viewing habits of female audiences watching the early evening British soap, *Crossroads*. Watching with the viewer-subject in their homes soon made her aware that their viewing experience was highly circumscribed by domestic demands. Women were simultaneously preoccupied with household duties, often only able to listen to the dialogue. It led Hobson to conclude that television viewing is defined by distraction. Her study also found that the women talked about the series as a whole (rather than limited to individual episodes), drawing on cultural knowledge and personal experience to interpret meaning. Furthermore, these female viewers extended their reading beyond what was actually depicted on screen. Her findings challenge Hall's preferred meanings model, suggesting instead that it is in the moment of reading where textual meaning is constructed. Hobson's model identifies audience discernment as the primary site of meaning production.

For feminist scholars of popular culture like Modleski, daytime soap opera mediates between the individual and society. Rather than dismiss this 'feminine' form as trivial and unworthy of serious critical attention, she aims to analyse what forms of pleasure such texts offer women. She turns to political science, psychoanalytic approaches to hysteria and reader response theories to gain insight into the complexities of the mediation process. Pleasures generated by daytime soap opera, argues Modleski, reveal a female viewer engaging with a surrogate extended family. Involved in the intimacies and intrigue of family life finds the woman taking pleasure in 'the fantasy of a fully self-sufficient family [beyond] her own isolated nuclear family' (1994: 108). Soap operas offer a 'collective fantasy – a fantasy of community but put in terms with which the viewer can be comfortable' (ibid.). Modleski recognises how the daytime soap opera meets real socio-cultural needs for women at home, however unsettling this may prove for feminists: '[It] is important to recognise that soap opera allays *real* anxieties, satisfies *real* needs and desires, even while it may distort them. The fantasy of community is not only a real desire (as opposed to the "false" ones mass culture is always accused of trumping up), it is a salutary one' (ibid.). Guided by feminist principles, Modleski contends that the significance of popular forms such as romance fiction and daytime soap operas lies in its complex relation involving fantasy and the everyday.

Questions of gendered pleasures, the interplay between reality and fiction, and television consumption are explored by Ien Ang (1996). Her 1985 ethnographic study of Dutch viewers watching the American top-rated soap opera, *Dallas*, offers an alternative interpretation of the text/reader relationship. She relies on letters from viewers to theorise the difficult relationship between feminism, women and a text appealing to female viewers. Analysing the diverse and often contradictory responses offered by women as to why they enjoyed watching *Dallas* leads her to construct a social analysis around pleasure and ideology. Female audiences emerge from this study as active, critical and selective. Yet, in contrast with audience research that privileges what people say as a direct reflection of their viewing experience without question, as Hobson's study does, Ang interprets the letters she received as 'texts':

> [The] letters must be regarded as texts, as discourses people produce when they want to express or have to account for their own preference for, or aversion to, a highly controversial piece of popular culture like *Dallas*. (1996: 11)

Searching for the 'socially available ideologies and images' beneath what is explicitly said in the letters allows her to put forward a model of television viewing based on how texts organise pleasure and ideological contexts mobilise meaning.

Drawing on Pierre Bourdieu's explanation of popular pleasure as 'characterised by an immediate emotional or sensual involvement in the object of pleasure' (1996: 20), Ang poses the question of what female audiences find pleasurable about *Dallas*? She identifies sources of pleasure located in the 'tension between the fictional and the real' (1996: 50) and the constant oscillation between female 'identification with and distancing from the fictional world' (ibid.) as well as in 'a structure of feeling which is aroused by the programme: the tragic structure of feeling' (1996: 47). Ang reveals how pleasure is associated not only with the cultural '*practice*' of watching *Dallas* but also a complex structure of feeling that is often hard to explain. Yet, however difficult it is to give an adequate explanation for those pleasures, it is clear to her that female viewing pleasures are not inevitably about women's social positioning as explained by orthodox psychoanalytic models but rather a product of women's everyday experience:

> They can 'lose' themselves in *Dallas* because the programme sym-
> bolises a structure of feeling which connects up with one of the
> ways in which they encounter life. And in so far as the imagination
> is an essential component of our psychological world, the pleasure
> of *Dallas* – as a historically specific symbolising of that imagination

      – is not a *compensation* for the presumed drabness of daily life,
      nor a *flight* from it, but a *dimension* of it. (1996: 83)

An important question raised by Ang's study is the role of the feminist researcher and her relationship with the 'ordinary' women under investigation. Her findings point to the theoretical problems confronting the feminist scholar reading female pleasures: 'A new antagonism is constructed here: that between the fantasies of powerlessness inscribed in the tragic structure of feeling, and the fantasies of protest and liberation inscribed in the feminist imagination' (1996: 132). Ang cautions feminists against 'the dangers of an over-politicising of pleasure' (ibid.). This charge of populism – meaning that no text can be criticised if enjoyed by a female audience – is echoed by Ellen Seiter, who notes, 'there is nothing inherently progressive about pleasure' (Seiter, Borchers, Kreutzner and Warth 1989: 5). Such comments reveal the dilemma facing feminist scholarship when attempting to rescue the female sub-cultural activity for theory and explain the enjoyment experienced by women audiences/readers, as well as the difficulties involved in what Charlotte Brunsdon calls the 'redemptive reading' of popular culture. What she means by this is the attempt made by feminist scholarship to identify the 'progressive' potential of the popular text as a means of countering 'both the left-pessimist despair over and the high-cultural dismissal of mass and popular culture' (1989: 121). Brunsdon makes known that 'redemptive reading' is motivated by a political impulse to bring feminist film theory into line with the experiences of real women.

    Reviewing 1980s feminist research, Brunsdon conveys her unease at the shift from the 'bad' text to the 'good' audience (1989: 125). She goes on to suggest that the media text has in fact been replaced 'by the text of the audience – a much more various and diverse text – and the enormous conceptual and methodological problem entailed' (1989: 122). Her conclusion here is that the empirical audience identified within ethnographical research is as much a theoretical construct as the textual spectator of psychoanalytic feminist theory (Mulvey 1999). What has happened in the effort to mask the disparity between the feminist scholar and ordinary female viewers/spectators, and give credence to the latter (as does Hobson whose work stands accused of relativism) is that ethnographic studies often fail to acknowledge the methodological problems involved. Ang later offers a response to this condemnation, in which she explains that this gap between the theoretical and political is embedded into the very project that is cultural studies:

> It is in the dialectic between the empirical and the theoretical, between experience and explanation, that forms of knowledge, that is interpretations, are constructed. Here, then, the thoroughly political nature of any research manifests itself. What is at stake is a *politics of interpretations*: 'to advance an interpretation is to insert it into a network of power relations ... audience ethnographies are undertaken because the relation between television and viewers is an empirical *question*. But the empirical is not the privileged domain of the *answers* ... Answers (temporary ones, to be sure) are to be constructed, in the form of interpretations'. (1989: 105–6)

Attempting to move on the debate about television audiences and research protocols finds Brunsdon making an important distinction between the textual subject constituted in the text and the 'social subject' constructed within culture (1981: 32). She rocognises how genres such as soap operas and the 'woman's film' aimed directly at female audiences are constituted primarily through 'the culturally constructed skills of femininity – sensitivity, perception, intuition and the necessary privileging of the concerns of the personal life' (1981: 36). These feminine texts position the subject within an ideological and institutional framework defined by family life and its attendant rituals – birth, engagement and marriage – which in turn assume that the imagined female viewer has the relevant cultural understanding. She concludes that such feminine texts appeal to the female television viewer as competent cultural readers. Her challenge to feminist film theory is to explore the interplay between the social reader and the social text.

Feminism and woman as cultural readers

Women's Pictures (1985) by Annette Kuhn is rooted in poststructuralist, psychoanalytic criticism and historical materialism. She puts forward a persuasive argument for a feminist film politics predicated on the idea that feminism makes known the mechanisms involved in producing knowledge about the social world. It leads her to claim that feminist film theory is itself another form of feminism, offering a vocabulary for understanding gendered representation and visual pleasures. The theories of the New French Feminisms (in fact Hélène Cixous' influential essay, 'Castration or Decapitation' was first translated by Kuhn for *Signs* in 1981) give her the means to suggest 'the possibility of a feminine text as one which would have no fixed formal "femininity" but could become feminine in the moment of reading' (Humm 1997: 28). The moment of reception and the question of readership are crucial to her work.

Kuhn tackles the text/context relation by first thinking about the differences between the spectator and the idea of the social audience. Each concept assumes particular meaning in relation 'to representations and to the context in which they are received' as well as requiring 'different methodologies and theoretical frameworks' (1992: 305) to understand how the individual relates to the film or television text. Whereas the spectator is constituted in and by the text, the social audience refers to the wider socio-cultural implications of going to the cinema or watching television: 'the concept of the social audience, as against that of spectator, emphasises the status of cinema and television as social and economic institutions' (ibid.). Unlike the spectator, those who buy a ticket to see a movie or sit at home viewing television 'can be surveyed, counted and categorised according to age, sex and socio-economic status' (ibid.). Kuhn distinguishes between the spectator and the social audience:

> The social audience becomes a spectator at the moment they engage in the processes and pleasures of meaning-making attendant on watching a film or television programme ... In taking part in the social act of consuming representations, a group of spectators becomes a social audience. (1992: 305–6)

Kuhn understands spectatorship as an act of readership. Meaning is not fixed in the text but instead is reconstituted through the process of reading. The text will be read in different ways, at different times and within different contexts. For her, there is difference between how gynocentric genres appeal to women in terms of how the female spectator is imagined by the producer, how she is constituted in the text and how the actual spectator is informed by or comes to resist these positionings. She calls on the scholar to study as discourse the interaction between text and context, between the woman as the imagined spectator (or textual subject) and woman as actual audience member (or social subject). She claims that academics must avoid collapsing the two positions into one another but instead consider the interaction between the two positions. Her 1984 essay, 'Women's Genres', in particular offers an attempt to rethink the social subject defined by those mentioned above like Brunsdon. Her article concludes that 'because texts do not operate in isolation from contexts, any answer to these questions [the relationship between text, context and female readers] must take into account the ways in which popular narratives are read, the conditions under which they are produced and consumed, and the ends to which they are appropriated (1992: 310).

'Pleasurable negotiations' and the female spectator

Feminist research into women's history and cultural forms identified the possibilities of resistant positions or deconstructive reading strategies. Christine Gledhill extends such thinking in her feminist inquiry into popular cultural forms and female spectatorship (1987; 1988). Her aim is to further bridge the theoretical gap identified by Kuhn between the textual subject and the social subject. Her interest focused on popular cultural forms such as the woman's picture, melodrama and soap opera, aimed at women commonly disparaged as having little or no cultural importance. Her work attempts to rescue these generic forms as well as challenge the assumptions of the psycho-linguistic and ideological approaches that define female spectatorship in terms of 'colonised, alienated or masochistic positions of knowledge' (1988: 66).

Gledhill contends that cultural forms are both a product and source of 'cultural negotiations', an ongoing process of cultural exchange – or what she calls 'give-and-take' (1988: 67). Meaning is not, she argues, 'imposed, nor passively imbibed' but 'arises out of a struggle or negotiation between competing frames of reference, motivation and experience' (1988: 68). Analysis of this 'negotiation' is achieved by looking at the constant contestation occurring across a number of competing sites: institutions (producers/directors), texts (films) and reception (audiences). Drawing on a number of principles rooted in neo-Marxism, semiotics and psychoanalysis 'while at the same time challenging the textual determinism and formalism of these approaches' (ibid.) allows Gledhill to claim that the work of ideology is far more fluid than the 1970s ideological analyses would have us believe. Instead ideology represents a site of perpetual struggle (based on the Gramscian model) involving a number of contesting voices with an investment in that structure: 'Language and cultural forms are sites in which different subjectivities struggle to impose or challenge, to confirm, negotiate or displace, definitions and identities' (1988: 72).

Of keen interest to Gledhill is how textual criticism can open up the question of 'woman' and 'distinguish the patriarchal *symbol* of "woman" from those discourses which speak from and to the historical socio-cultural experience of "women"' (1988: 75). What her work on melodrama for example reveals is a 'struggle between male and female voices over the meaning of the symbol "woman"' (1987: 37). Of the representation of woman, she contends that if woman is a sign then it does not go uncontested. Instead it is fought over by competing social groupings with a stake in the struggle. A textual analysis of *Coma* (Michael Crichton, 1977) enables her to reveal the figure of the woman at the core of cultural negotiations taking place. She identifies that the text is conditioned by two co-existing discourses – melodrama and realism – that enable it 'to work both on a symbolic, "imaginary" level, internal to fictional production and on a "realist" level, referring to the socio-historical world outside the text' (1988: 75). Melodrama contributes 'Manichaean moral frameworks' with known archetypes and polemic struggles while realism 'grounds the drama in a recognisable verisimilitude' (1988: 76). Analysing the figure of the woman realises the contested field of gender discourse, a negotiation between 'woman' as patriarchal symbol and a feminist cultural history involving real women:

> The image of the woman has ... been a site of gendered discourse, drawn from the specific social-cultural experience of women and shared by women, which negotiates a space within, and sometimes resists, patriarchal domination. At the same time new definitions of gender and sexuality circulated by the women's movement contest the value and meaning of the female image, struggling for different, female recognitions and identifications. (Ibid.)

The role of the 'textual critic' is identified by Gledhill as key to analysing 'the *conditions and possibilities of reading*' (1988: 74). Of importance to Gledhill is the role of the feminist critic and the 'dual operation' she must perform. In the first instance the critic utilises textual analysis to reveal 'the conditions and possibilities of gendered reading', to open out the text and expose the cultural negotiation taking place around woman as sign. Yet on another level, the feminist textual analysis will 'put into circulation readings that draw the text into a female and/or feminist orbit' (1988: 75). Certain meanings associated with gender identity and sexual difference will prove more significant than others for the feminist. This is further complicated because what is important for one feminist may not prove so interesting for another. As a result, these different feminist readings create another layer to the text as a contested site of meaning: 'In this way traditions are broken and remade [and] critical activity itself participates in social negotiation of meaning, definition and identity' (1988: 74).

Psychic investments, historical audiences and female spectatorship

Jackie Stacey looks to reconcile what she sees as the incompatibility between feminist film theory and cultural studies audience research by aiming to offer a corrective to earlier models and put the 'spectators back into theories of female spectatorship' (1994: 76). Grounding her research in an ethnographical study of the viewing habits and cultural experience of British female movie-goers during World War Two and the post-war period finds her analysing material collected from female respondents about their memories of Hollywood cinema and its stars. The complexities of the spectator/star relationship arising from her findings lead her to consider 'the ways in which psychic investments are grounded within specific sets of historical and cultural relations which in turn shape the formation of identities on conscious and unconscious levels' (1994: 79).

Stacey begins by surveying psychoanalytic theories on the female image, cinematic spectatorship and visual pleasure to identify the issues that she wishes to address. Given that our 'culture [is] saturated with images of desirable femininity' (1994: 124), and that women imbibe such images and are positioned to constantly reproduce them, means she must rethink current thinking about 'how women look at feminine ideals on the cinema screen' (1994: 16). Broadening the scope of her study to combine psychoanalytic theories on desire and identification with considerations of historical and social formations grounds her interpretation of the data drawn from responses received to an advertisement she placed in two women's magazines, *Woman's Realm* and *Woman's Weekly*. Letters were followed up with a questionnaire compiled from the initial responses.

Stacey notes that her respondents originate from a narrow socio-economic grouping – all were white and belonged to C1, C2 and D social classes. Acknowledging the limitations imposed by this leads her to conclude that this ethnographic research on the relationship between *female* spectators and *female* Hollywood stars from the 1940s and 1950s remains primarily 'a study of white fantasy and the relationships between white female spectators and their ideals on the Hollywood screen' (1994: 62). It also allows her to assert the politics of location – the importance of historical and national specificities – when considering theories of female spectatorship.

Stacey identified in the material three key discourses of spectatorship: escapism, identification and consumption. Each is investigated to reveal the complex image-making processes involved in producing dominant constructions of femininity at that time but also how Hollywood stars offered female spectators the fantasy of becoming the ideal. The utopian feelings of 'abundance, community and transcendence' (1994: 124) generated by cinematic constructions of femininity structure escapist fantasies for the female respondents. Fantasies of escape are not only rooted in the British wartime experience of real loss and economic hardship but are also about gendered cultural processes that give women the opportunity to temporarily merge with a more ideal femininity that is both energising and restricting. Looking at how female spectators consumed star identities prompts Stacey to explore how discourses of consumption offered 'women the possibility of the production of self and of agency in the public sphere' (1994: 223) beyond traditional feminine identities and roles as wives and mothers. It further enables her to claim that such text-audience encounters allowed for the possibility of transforming oneself. Self-transformation helped women to negotiate an unsettling and austere present during wartime, and to resist the post-war conservative drive to dragoon them back into the home while responding to the new consumer boom and 'Americanisation' of British culture.

Sections on identification/identity involved in the production of pleasure make it possible for her to combine psychoanalytic theory with an historical approach to audience research. Tracing multiple processes of identification and desire that connect the female spectator to the star, she identifies two broad categories: 'identificatory fantasies and identificatory practices' (1994: 171). While identificatory fantasies (like devotion, adoration, worship) involve the pleasurable feelings experienced by the female spectator while looking at the star, identificatory practices (such as resembling, imitating, coping) refer to extra-cinematic practices involving pro-active self-transformation. Identificatory practices not only entail private fantasies but also motivate cultural activities such as copying dress and hairstyles, using a similar cosmetic, smoking a cigarette or adopting a particular way of talking. The female spectator indulges in a self-conscious play with feminine identities, in which 'the star's identity is selectively reworked and incorporated into the spectator's new identity' (ibid.). But this is not simply about passive acceptance. Rather it is 'an active engagement and production of changing identities' (1994: 172). Identifying how processes of cinematic spectatorship construct and transform feminine identities leads her to conclude that the relationship between stars and spectators involved 'a complex negotiation between self and other, image and ideal, subject and object. Screen image and self image are connected through a dialectical interplay of multiple feminine identities' (1994: 227).

To open out this complex question of star/spectator relations, Stacey turns to 'object-relations theory' associated with Melanie Klein. Klein's theory of 'projection' and 'introjection' explains the mechanisms involved in how a child learns to deal with the external world:

> Projection is a process whereby states of feeling and unconscious wishes are expelled from the self and attributed to another person or thing. Introjection is a process whereby qualities that belong to an external object are absorbed and unconsciously regarded as belonging to the self. (Klein, quoted in Stacey 1994: 229)

Object-relations theory, with its understanding of subject formation based on an interaction with external others, provides Stacey with a useful model to interrogate looking relations, desire and identification. It enables her to reveal that identity formation is never complete but rather an on-going process of negotiation and reformation. It also provides her with the means to describe the 'multiple dialectical replays between spectator and star, between self and ideal other' (1994: 231). Yet to guard against the universalising tendencies inherent within psychoanalytic models, she insists that the theory must be combined with an analysis of how modes of cinematic perception are subject to 'broader historical transformations' and linked to specific cultural and historical locations (1994: 240).

Black female spectatorship and resistant viewing practices

Jacqueline Bobo (1988; 1993; 1995), bell hooks (1992; 1993) and Michele Wallace (1993; 1997) have tackled the issue of Black female spectatorship within a cultural studies framework. Pre-eminent here is the cultural criticism and ethnographic studies which address the ignorance surrounding the Black female spectator and her viewing experience. Bobo calls on her colleagues to understand the social and cultural experience of this underrepresented group: 'Unfortunately, when the female spectator is usually spoken of and spoken for, the female in question is white and middle class. As a Black woman working within the discipline of cultural studies, my goal is to expand the scholarship on the female spectator beyond this' (1989: 101–2). Black feminism aimed to open out the debate and consider the Black female spectator, both as an empirical group and a theoretical concept.

hooks investigates viewing strategies developed by Black female spectators in opposition to what is expected within mainstream popular culture. She begins by arguing that white supremacist patriarchy is institutionalised through the maintenance of derogatory stereotypes that continue to oppress and exploit all Black people. In particular, she notes how the Black female spectator's presence is conceived of as absence, and the Black female body on screen is denied in favour of her Caucasian counterpart in order to preserve white phallocentric looking relations. Asking a Black female spectator about why Black female spectatorship suffers neglect, hooks was met with the following reply: 'We are afraid to talk about ourselves as spectators because we have been so abused by the "gaze"' (1993: 297).

By interrogating the politics of racially constructed looking in the American context, hooks identifies the violence suffered by Black people through the gaze. She situates this mistreatment within the politics of slavery and racialised power relations in which slaves were denied the right to look (1992; 1993). Grounding her thinking in Foucauldian terms about dominant power-producing disciplinary strategies through regimes of observation and surveillance enables her to claim how subjugated Black peoples' 'right to gaze had produced ... an overwhelming longing to look, a rebellious desire, an oppositional gaze' (1993: 288–9). She states that Black people resist dominant structures of looking, and instead seize on the opportunity to look differently.

Offered no space within a visual economy defined by the male gaze and an idealised image of white femininity means the Black female spectator develops a critical or 'oppositional gaze' 'where cinematic visual delight is the pleasure of interrogation' (1992: 126). Such an oppositional gaze has evolved from the experience of racial and sexist discrimination (a product of Black history and personal experience) and has resulted in a resistant consciousness. It is a gaze built up through resistance against mainstream media texts that produce and institute images which either deny Black women (the woman as absent), or constructs stereotypical images of Black woman as the non-feminine Other (an image situated within a binary opposition to an idealised white femininity). For the Black female spectator, refusal to align with the phallocentric gaze allows for a critical space to open up in which binary oppositions can be challenged and critiqued, and where negative images can possibly be reclaimed. For these spectators, visual pleasure can be distanced and interrogative. But hooks recognises that Black female spectatorship is even more complex than this model suggests, for while the resistant critical gaze is a product of personal and historical experience, it is not guaranteed by it. A Black female spectator may for example possess a colonised gaze, one in fact informed by dominant modes of colonial looking and decoding.

Jacqueline Bobo picks up on similar concerns about resistant spectating practices and the Black female spectator as cultural readers in her work. Noting that little attention is paid to 'Black female cultural consumers' (1995: 1), she identifies a critical ignorance surrounding how Black women use and make sense of media texts. Accepting Kuhn's model of the spectator and the social audience, and extending further Gledhill's concept of 'negotiation', she undertakes ethnographic studies of Black women viewers to 'examine the way in which a specific audience creates meaning from a mainstream text and uses the reconstructed meaning to empower themselves and their social group' (1988: 93). Her most famous study focused on Black women's reaction to Steven Spielberg's 1985 film adaptation of Alice Walker's novel, *The Color Purple*. Conducting a series of interviews with Black female spectators gives her insight into why, despite Spielberg's use of traditional racial stereotypes and the overwhelmingly negative publicity received by the film from the Black press, Black women reacted extremely positively to the film – and even felt empowered by it.

I have found that on the whole Black women have discovered something progressive and useful in the film. It is crucial to understand how this is possible when viewing a work made according to the encoding of dominant ideology. Black women's responses to *The Color Purple* loom as an extreme contrast to those of many other viewers. Not only is the difference in reception noteworthy but Black women's responses confront and challenge a prevalent method of media audience analysis which insists that viewers of mainstream works have no control or influence over a cultural product. (1988: 95)

Rethinking Stuart Hall's encoding/decoding model (described earlier) enables Bobo to suggest how this marginalised group of women constructed their own meanings from the film. 'Out of habit, as readers of mainstream texts, we have learned to ferret out the beneficial and put up blinders against the rest' (1988: 96).

Bobo's definition of resistance as a reading strategy for these women is indebted to the efforts of other Black feminist cultural historians (Barbara Christian, Darlene Hill) and literary scholars (Patricia Hill Collins). Taking from these academics a context for understanding Black female experience as being about historical disenfranchisement, invisibility and defiance leads her to argue that Black female cultural readers bring along with them to the cinema personal histories and an awareness of the history of demeaning representations of Black women. Such cultural consumption is further shaped by the recent renaissance in Black women's poetry, fiction and autobiography concerned with 'the personal lives and collective histories of Black women' (1988: 104). Her conclusions here are shaped by what David Morley calls 'interdiscourse' (1980a) – that is, the encounter between the text and reader/spectator. This moment of textual encounter – or what she calls 'cultural competency' – is one whereby the reader/spectator brings with them a range of other knowledges specific to their cultural background 'to the act of watching a film and creating meaning from a work' (1988: 102–3). As Bobo sees it, the positive readings made by Black women of *The Color Purple*, with its negative stereotypes, reveals a community of women used to filtering out derogatory racist images and adapting mainstream texts 'to give new meaning' (1988: 105) to their own lives as Black women: 'This community of heightened consciousness is in the process of creating new self images and forming a force for change' (1988: 107).

Bobo draws heavily on cultural studies methodologies and extensively quotes from her interviews with Black women spectators to support her thesis that Black viewing pleasures are about an inter-textual cultural experience. Yet the role of the critic is key to unlocking meaning about that experience. The actual female spectator belonging to the social audience becomes reconstituted as a theoretical construction in the process of Bobo interpreting what is said and linking her findings to wider socio-historical realities related to Black women. The Black feminist critic not only participates in the discussion group but also acts as a kind of interpreter, 'to give voice to those who are usually never considered in any analysis of cultural works' (1995: 51). In the process of deciphering what is being said, she can help Black women make sense of a uniquely Black women's perspective which their collective experience has revealed but might not seem so obvious.

Michele Wallace points to the difficulties involved in theorising invisibility for the Black female spectator. While it is a debate around gender and race that is more fully realised in chapter three, what is relevant here is her concern with questions of female spectatorship and identification. Her work interrogates how Black female spectators (especially given that African-Americans spent around $150 million a year on movies in 1943) made sense of Hollywood stereotyping. What is most striking about her work is how she inserts her voice and personal experience into her theoretical analysis of sexist and racist conventions in Hollywood films. She speaks eloquently of growing up watching classical Hollywood movies (1993: 263). In particular she recalls how the stars (what they wore, their hairstyles and demeanour) and the narratives became 'important cultural currency' (ibid.) for the women of her family. Claiming to have identified with both Joan Crawford ('it was always said amongst Black women that Joan Crawford was part Black' (1993: 264)) *and* Hattie McDaniels ('the bumbling, lazy, Black, asexual and childlike female' (1993: 262–3)) in *Mildred Pearce* (Michael Curtiz, 1944) prompts her to ponder the question of how Black female spectators take possession of dominant representation and make sense of it: 'The process may have been about problematising and expanding one's racial identity instead of abandoning it. It seems crucial here to view spectatorship not only as potentially bisexual but also multiracial and multiethnic' (1993: 264). She concludes by assessing the significance of Julie Dash's 1991 film, *Daughters in the Dust* – a film that chronicles two days in the life of the Peazant family. What Wallace argues is that these representations of Black women correct a neglect for Black audiences, 'reformulating notions of spectatorship to encompass the impact of "race" on subjectivity' (1997: 101).

Lesbian as social subject

Tasmin Wilton is adamant that scholars must 'make space in film studies and cultural studies for the specificity of lesbian thinking, lesbian oppression and lesbian resistance' and 'to understand lesbian spectatorship as a constant struggle to insist on and locate "lesbian" as a reading/viewing position' (1995: 3, 157). While the theoretical challenge posed by lesbian/queer studies to the hegemony of traditional hetero-binarism will be explored in more detail in chapter four, what is important here is the contribution made to understanding processes of spectatorship. Working from a cultural studies perspective, she rejects psychoanalytic theory for beating genders and sexual identities into a 'square hole' (1995: 157). Instead she proposes 'the notion of the *cinematic contract*' (1995: 16), by which she means 'the spectator agrees to draw upon the personal emotional/political/social narratives which she brings with her into the cinema in order to devise engagement strategies which she puts at the service of the film' (1995: 151).

Mainstream cultural hostility toward the lesbian subject and lesbian-ism is a social reality, argues Wilton, in which 'women who identify as "lesbian" inhabit a particular set of interstices among social notions of gender, desire, deviance, criminality, sin, naturalness' (1995: 158–9). The lesbian brings along her own 'personal and social narratives of oppression' to the cinema and uses them 'to construct engagement strategies with which to make meaning of the film' (1995: 159). Sitting in the cinema finds the lesbian either experiencing an 'adversarial engagement' (1995: 151), as she works hard to locate pleasure in a text that does not want her 'to watch with lesbian eyes' (1995: 148), or setting 'aside entirely [a] lesbian reading position' (1995: 156). Pleasure comes from a 'temporary escape' from socio-political and gendered identities.

Andrea Weiss cautions scholars against assuming a 'coherent, unified position of identification among all lesbians, despite wide cultural, racial, class and generational differences' (1992: 3). Her work combines theories of the social subject with psychoanalytic models to offer a sophisticated reading of lesbian spectatorship. Focusing on Hollywood stars and lesbian spectatorship in 1930s and 1940s Hollywood, she describes how subjugated, alternative identities were recouped by a gay subculture from dominant discourses and cultural practices. At the height of the studio era, the Hollywood star system 'created inconsistent images of femininity' (1998: 286) while auxiliary texts circulated details of the stars' 'real lives' to create a lesbian network of innuendo and gossip. Looking at stars like Marlene Dietrich, Greta Garbo and Katharine Hepburn, Weiss explains how these 'extraordinary' actresses intervened into 'the process of star image production' and 'often asserted gestures and movements in their films that were inconsistent with and even posed an ideological threat' to heterosexual narrative closure (1998: 286–7). Detailing the ways in which the Hollywood star system distanced the lesbian spectator from the 'lesbian' star (the 1934 Motion Picture Code prohibited representations of homosexuality; Hollywood films constructed the 'lesbian' star as exotic Other) with what was said about the 'mannish lesbian' in contemporary public discourses (scientific journals, women's fiction) allows Weiss to contend that 'identification involves both conscious and unconscious processes' and 'varying degrees of subjectivity and distance depending on race, class and sexual difference' (1998: 291). Lesbian spectatorship involves, she argues, a complex process of negotiation between the private fantasies of the individual lesbian spectator, the sexually ambiguous and androgynous qualities that stars like Dietrich and Garbo exhibited, and extra-cinematic discourses (rumours relating to a star's sexual orientation) that authorise lesbian readings.

Film history, cultural memory and the historical female spectator

Broadening understanding of cultural studies as a methodology can be seen in the work of those engaged in producing a feminist historiography of early cinema. Patrice Petro describes the two distinctive branches of film historiographies as 'a history of film as institutionally and formally pro-duced (the history of film as a privileged object) and a history of film as it is received in culture (the history of the spectator-subject)' (2002: 32). The urgency felt in recovering women's participation, as producers, directors, stars and writers as well as spectators and consumers, in shaping cinema parallel a perceived crisis in academic film feminism (Bean 2002: 2–3). Coinciding with its seeming decline and sense of 'a lost (female) object' (ibid.) finds female scholars occupied in an energetic pursuit that has only recently started to survey films believed to be lost and cultural documents previously overlooked. Demonstrating a commitment to archival research and interdisciplinary frameworks, and analysing film prints using a diverse array of inherited documents (censorship reports, fan magazines, advertisement, audiences studies) means the recent feminist interest into early cinema has provided a new direction for film feminism. Feminist historiographies seek to locate the institution of cinema and its female spectators within wider socio-cultural contexts, linked to such factors as consumer habits and leisure patterns, censorship and cinema reform; in so doing, feminist cultural film histories have contributed with new historical knowledge and with new methodological approaches to the study of film and film history.

Work undertaken by Miriam Hansen (1984; 1990; 1991), Anne Friedberg (1993) and Giuliana Bruno (1993) challenge our thinking about early cinema and the female spectator, to suggest far more complex modes of film consumption. Identifying early cinema as a new kind of proletarian sphere designed to appeal to the masses prompts Hansen in particular to claim that it offered the potential for re-organising public experience, especially for those social groups such as women whom official forces previously ignored: 'These groups had either no access to existing institutions of public life or, in the case of women, only in a highly regulated and dependent form' (1991: 91). That the empirical data from the era reveals 'patterns of interaction between the film industry and its audience, both of [which were] determined by a capitalist mode of production' (1983: 176) leads her to conclude that women were attracted to the cinema precisely because it presented a radically new kind of public sphere for them. As Hansen claims, 'more than any other entertainment form, the cinema opened up a space – a social space as well as a perceptual, experimental horizon – in women's lives' (1991: 117).

Identifying historically distinct modes of pleasurable female looking has consumed various women scholars keen to dispute the ahistorical female subject central to psychoanalytic thinking (Mulvey 1975; 1999). Casting a critical eye over the appeal Rudolph Valentino held for female spectators in the 1920s through combining Freudian and feminist film theory (on the gaze and female spectatorship) with empirical evidence (studio-produced publicity and press reports), Hansen reads that the cult of Valentino complete with adorning fans as unique: 'Never before was the discourse on fan behaviour so strongly marked by the terms of sexual difference, and never again was spectatorship so explicitly linked to the discourse on female desire' (2000: 226). Other female film historians like Gaylyn Studlar (1996) have read the representation of Valentino as an object of erotic contemplation for female audiences. Such pleasure constructed in and beyond (notably fan magazines) the film text reveals to both scholars how the Valentino image spoke about apparent changes in female sexual and social identities. Studying industrial strategies – how Valentino's star image was constructed in film and presented to the public through publicity – gives us insight into how female desire is constructed in terms of industrial demands, consumerism and visual pleasures.

Other scholars (Bean & Negra 2002) propose new historiographies of the female spectator. Such diverse research provides insight into issues of historical, social, national and local specificities shaping what might be called a historical spectator. Lauren Rabinovitz, investigating the 'temptations' offered by the moviegoing experience, notes how Nickelodeons (the first purpose-built cinemas) 'invited women to find sensual pleasure in their own bodies and simultaneously transformed them into spectacles ... [they] helped to construct female sexual identity among these women' (1990: 71). Dressing up in fashionable styles to visit leisure sites like the cinema appealed to the social aspirations of working-class women, argues Kathy Peiss (1986). Buying stylish clothes and wearing cosmetics enabled working women to transform themselves, albeit briefly, through consumption and exhibitionism. More recent accounts offered by Constance Balides, Kristine Butler and Lori Landay (cited in Bean & Negra 2002) contribute further to our understanding of women's visual and physical mobility in early-twentieth-century urban centres. Combining a focus on the new forms of womanhood – the *flâneuse*, the flapper – promoted at the cinema with new inter-disciplinary frameworks and historical evidence enables them to tease out different theoretical approaches and fresh discussions on female empowerment and feminine scopophilic desire (see Butler in Bean & Negra 2002), on how modern lifestyles for women were regulated (Balides in Bean & Negra 2002) or how new representations of femininity linked social and physical mobility with new mobile ways to looking and desiring (Landy in Bean & Negra 2002).

Grounding her contribution in contemporary cultural debates about cinema and its audience as well as industrial practices that courted female patrons, Shelley Stamp (1996; 2000) reveals that women's relationship to the motion picture culture between 1905 and into the 1910s is more complex than previously suggested. Cinema's attempt to elevate its cultural status coincides with its campaign to build a female audience. Women, especially middle-class women, personified respectability which cinema sought for itself: 'social propriety, refined manners and impeccable taste' (Stamp 2000: 6); 'Ladies were courted with matinee screenings, commodious service', promotions, and other theatre schemes 'encouraging them to integrate cinema-going into their daily routines of shopping, socialisation and child-rearing' (2000: 10). Absorbing them into the genteel culture cinema also involved teaching women not only how to be modern but also how to conduct themselves.

Analysing the white slave films popular with female audiences during the 1910s leads Stamp to conclude that the 'competing discourses that surround these films – about commercial recreation, female patrons and movie morals – reveal the degree to which women's film-going remained entangled with sexual danger in the 1910s' (2000: 100). Investigating the controversy surrounding these vice movies as well as wider public concerns about white slavery (about white women sold into prostitution) reveals to her how these white slave films tapped into inherent fears about women's increased involvement in urban leisure culture. It makes known a gap between an industry keen to court female patronage and its grappling with the implications of a female spectatorship evidently drawn to these vice films.

Like white slave narratives, serial forms featuring plucky heroines like *Perils of Pauline*, *Hazards of Helen* or *Exploits of Elaine* gave representation to new freedoms for women. Not only does the serial heroine represent an industrial attempt to cultivate a female fan base based around a commodity (a series of films, stars, fan magazines) but also a paradox in what these film products had to say about modern womanhood beyond marriage and home: 'Pleasing though these fantasies of independence might have been for contemporary viewers, they were invariably laced with peril, for even as the absence of family ties frees serial heroines to enjoy lives of adventure, it usually also places them in grave danger' (2000: 129).

Interdisciplinary in her approach, and combining archival research into film melodrama and illustrated magazines with theoretical debates, Petro (1989) looks at representations of women in mass Weimar culture during the 1920s. This feminist revision of Weimar film history conceptualises female spectatorship as rooted in historical specific representational practices (illustrated magazines, films, advertising) that defy strict binary oppositions. Work undertaken by Janet Staiger (1995) on regulating female sexuality in the 1910s, and Lea Jacob's study (1997) on censorship practices shaping female representation during the classical Hollywood period put forward further models for thinking about how female bodies and sexuality were policed by the cinema.

Romantic comedy and gender

Another burgeoning field of study involving cultural theories and film feminism relates to romantic comedy, gender representation and visual pleasures. Certain sub-genres have become privileged sites of discussion around text, context and the spectator/viewer. Screwball comedy from the 1930s for example is interpreted by scholars such as Tina Olsin Lent (1995) as centring on a negotiation of changing conceptions of courtship, love and romance, and wedlock at a time when the institution of marriage was perceived in a state of crisis.

Television comedy is another area of recent feminist inquiry, which investigates in particular star performance, joke-making techniques and the television audience. Alexander Doty (1990), investigating the interplay between the star image of Lucille Ball and the character she plays in *I Love Lucy* (Desilu Productions Inc/CBS, 1951–57) argues that Lucy Ricardo is constructed as the zany, loveable, ditzy and talentless housewife and mother based on the denial, repression and (re)construction of Ball's star image. Patricia Mellencamp (1997) is another scholar fascinated by Lucille Ball's slapstick routines. Recuperating Ball's performance as an act of defiance from the confinement of the domestic space allows her to locate the radical underpinnings of the show for female viewers. Each week finds Lucy unsuccessfully attempting to escape domesticity and break into show business. The physical comic routines performed by Ball offered a means of challenging patriarchy as she upstages her husband/other men; and this is what audiences tuned in to see. Drawing on Freud's theory of humorous pleasures (that is, humour used to avoid emotional pain) enables Mellencamp to argue that laughter directed at Lucy's performance of being talentless – 'her wretched, off-key singing, her mugging facial exaggerations and out-of-step dancing [is] paradoxically both the source of the audience's pleasure and the narrative necessity for housewifery' (1997: 73). She contends that Lucy's situation made visible the real dilemmas faced by many women: 'Given the repressive conditions of the 1950s, humour might have been women's weapon and tactic of survival, ensuring sanity, the triumph of the ego, and pleasures' (ibid).

One of the most sustained discussions on gender, representation and cross-cultural theories is Kathleen Rowe's study of the unruly woman (1995). Using theoretical models from Mikhail Bakhtin concerned with the grotesque, Rowe identifies the grotesque body as ultimately the female body – often an outrageous, voluptuous, loud, joke-cracking dissenter or 'woman on top'. The unruly female is not about gender confusion but inverting dominant social, cultural and political conventions; unruliness occurs when those who are socially or politically inferior (normally, women) use humour and excess to undermine patriarchal norms and authority. Focusing on Roseanne Arnold allows her to suggest how Roseanne's star image and her television situation (Carsey-Werner Company/ABC, 1988–1997) disrupt and expose the gap between feminist liberation (informed by second-wave feminism) and the realities of working-class family life (those of whom feminist liberation left behind), between ideals of true womanhood and unruliness to challenge notions of a patriarchal construction of femininity. Making a spectacle of herself – her overweight body, her physical excesses, her performance as loud and brash – reveals ambivalence as the unruly woman speaks out. Difficulties faced by Roseanne in the press with the vitriol directed at her 'make known the problems of representing what in our culture still remains largely unrepresentable: a fat woman who is also sexual; a sloppy housewife who's a good mother; a "loose" woman who is also tidy, who hates matrimony but loves her husband, who hates the ideology of true womanhood, yet considers herself a domestic goddess' (1995: 91).

As I hope is clear, feminist critics disclose how television culture is informed by context and given meaning through the ways in which particular programmes are consumed, how narratives are experienced and what they mean to the female viewer – what television series says about women and how media texts function in their daily lives. Through interviews, Deborah Jermyn (2003) analyses how women talk about the series in an effort to understand what *Sex and the City* (HBO, 1998–2004) means to female fans. Pivotal here is the point at which Jermyn's own fandom intersects with the experience of those she interviewed – it is a moment that allows her to reveal both the pleasures and difficulties involved in understanding how fan culture operates and how to speak about it.

Feminists working in the field of cultural studies contributed with a critical shift from the text as the primary site of meaning to the dynamic and complex interaction between institutions, text and consumer. Whereas feminists rooted in semiotic and psychoanalytic approaches understand spectatorship as being about textual address with meaning produced by the text, cultural studies conversely understands spectatorship as about a process of negotiation involving producer, text and spectator in which meaning is made in the act of readership. Identifying the materiality of the female audience and the social experience of spectatorship seemed to offer a way out of the impasse created by semiotic-psychoanalytic film theory. Cultural studies approaches made a significant contribution to the re-evaluation of popular pleasures and furthered our thinking about the processes of spectatorship.

The shift to understand popular culture and its audiences as a site of negotiation/contestation nevertheless proves unsettling for some female scholars. Meaghan Morris noted back in 1988 that cultural studies was going through a 'banal' period. What she refers to here is the impoverishment of current theory to talk about contemporary media texts. Concerns are also raised over interpreting a text when meaning is up for grabs (Tasker 1991: 96), and over attempts to reclaim the popular as (politically) progressive (Modleski 1986: xii; Brunsdon 1989: 125). What ethnographic work on contemporary audiences as well as textual studies of television fictions like *Roseanne* and *Sex and the City* reveals is that feminism is a word that cannot be uttered. A postfeminist return to where women freely choose traditional romance and social roles has placed pressure on the academy to locate different analytic tools to understand these filmic and television texts.

Redemptive readings pioneered by female cultural studies scholars took on a feminine form. In part related to a broader acceptance of feminism as a critical discourse (Modleski 1991: 3), and in part due to the cultural studies articulation of the feminine as about disruption, resistance became gendered. Feminine viewing practices and female genres/texts were appropriated by a body of male criticism eager to analyse male power, male hegemony and masculinity (Neale 1983; Cohen & Hark 1993). Assimilation of the 'feminine' into academic (male) thinking has widened our knowledge about gender identity and sexual difference within a postfeminist context but feminists like Tania Modleski urge us to be cautious for 'male power frequently works to efface female subjectivity by occupying the site of femininity' (1991: 7).

Despite methodological queries and intellectual difficulties raised in several studies, the interdisciplinary endeavour to generate a dialogue between psychoanalytic theory, ethnologic studies and theories related to historical and socio-cultural formations proves tremendously productive. The text no longer determines meaning but instead is produced through complex processes of negation and contestation involving producers and consumers.

RACE, ETHNICITY AND POST-COLONIALISM/MODERNISM

Feminist inquiry into race and representation grew out of a wider encounter between feminism and postmodernism – emerging in the late 1980s
– linked to debates initiated by Jean-François Lyotard (*The Postmodern
Condition*, translated in 1984) and Fredric Jameson ('Postmodernism, or
the Cultural Logic of Late Capitalism', also published in 1984). Barbara
Creed examines the impact of postmodernism on the feminist academy,
and in particular the influence of Lyotard's theory of the collapse of grand
narratives which 'have been used to legitimate the quest for knowledge
and the importance of scientific research' (1987: 50). Questioning the
legitimacy of master narratives and their signifying practices, along with
changing post-colonial attitudes toward ethnic groups and cultural identities in the wake of 1960s liberation movements (civil rights, anti-Vietnam
war protests), undermined the position of Western institutions as a site
of 'truth' and power. Identifying feminist interventions into discussions
on race, this chapter charts how scholars disrupt master narratives and
orthodox (white) feminism to produce new truths about female subjectivity, representation and experience.

Interrogating the historical invisibility and theoretical elision of women
of colour took on a new emphasis within the context of a postmodern discourse – questioning the hegemonic nature of dominant narratives and
who had the right to speak. It led scholars to think about the conditions
in which knowledge about race and gender is made possible. Such a dialogue was anticipated some years earlier by second-wave feminism and its
critique of patriarchy. However, whereas Claire Johnston and Laura Mulvey
felt that female absence within the signifying processes of mainstream

(patriarchal) cinema was lamentable, feminists influenced by postmodern thinking identified the theoretical possibilities in those very spaces over which the dominant patriarchal fiction had lost control. This opened up new avenues of inquiry based on the possibilities afforded by resistance, absence and uncertainty which were constituted in Black feminist literary criticism, histories of slavery and the colonial imagination as well as post-colonialism and revisions of psychoanalytic paradigms. Focusing on the crisis of narrative allowed feminists to take up a number of important issues – questions to do with who has the right to speak about another, systems of knowledge and a belief about the world within which the power to define the Other is constituted, and the desire to think differently linked to the postmodern concept of 'hybridity'. I begin by setting this debate on race and representation in context by identifying key problems as well as methodologies which helped film feminism unlock questions of ethnic difference, represenation and subjectivity.

An oppressive orthodoxy

'I know nothing about her.' (Fanon 1986: 180)

Orthodox feminist application of psychoanalytic models based on a rigid binary understanding of subject formation increasingly came under scrutiny from *within* the feminist academy. For those concerned with race, these theories failed to account for racial and sexual difference beyond the closed Oedipal world. bell hooks in particular felt that the orthodox feminist approach, 'rooted in an ahistorical psychoanalytic framework, silenced racial difference – of a racialised sexual difference' (1993: 295). Others condemned the psychoanalytic approach for its deficiencies as a methodology to account for complex historical encounters involving gender and race (Bobo 1989; Mercer 1994; Young 1996; Gaines 2000).

Understanding how patriarchy constitutes power to oppress all women underpins the orthodox thinking – and caused the critical impasse. Rooted in a Marxist dialectic of class struggle and economic divisions of labour, Marxist feminist analysis could not conceive of categories beyond those defined by a strict binary structure – male/female, active/passive. Specifics of gender identity and race became elided in favour of a broader ideological agenda that reference sexual difference in terms of male power and female subordination. But it soon became apparent to scholars that oppression of and against women did not operate in the same way. Hazel Carby for example identifies that Black women fit somewhat awkwardly into the traditional Marxist feminist paradigm based on a strict gender divide under patriarchy:

> The fact that Black women are subject to the *simultaneous* oppression of patriarchy, class and 'race' is the prime reason for not employing parallels that render their position and experience not only marginal but also invisible. (1982: 213)

Her remarks confirm what other feminists were saying about a 'fundamental antagonism' (Gaines 2000: 341) embedded within orthodox Marxist feminism, in which it was almost impossible to think about difference beyond gender conflict. Jane Gaines sums up the frustration for feminists at this critical moment in the early 1980s: 'the oppression of *women* of colour remains incompletely grasped by the classical paradigm' (ibid.).

Attempts to understand the theoretical difficulties revealed an unconscious institutional oppression within the feminist discourse: namely, a style of thought involving white feminism and the Black woman. hooks contends that in the effort to understand the inferior status accorded women under patriarchy, the orthodoxy silenced, and even erased, nonwhite women from film analysis as it claimed the right to speak for them, 'as though it speaks about "women" when in actuality it speaks only about White women (1993: 295). Only speaking about Caucasian females means that the Black woman becomes lost:

> [The] category of women is usually used to refer to white women, while the category of Blacks often really means 'Black men'. What is lost in the process is the situation of the Black woman. Her position becomes quite peculiar and oppressively unique: in terms of oppression, she is both Black and a woman; in terms of theory, she is neither. In effect, she occupies a position which is difficult to think within current paradigms. (Doane 1991: 231)

Implied here is the idea that the Black woman has no institutional Other within orthodox binary structures (hooks 1992); she is the institutional Other to the Black man but she has no Other for herself. The non-white woman emerged as theoretically invisible from inside the feminist academy through its failure to identify political allegiances based on race rather than gender (Joseph 1981; Combahee River Collective 1986) and its tendency to foreground one site of contestation (gender) at the expense of misinterpreting another (race). Feminist film scholars investigating these questions would look beyond their own discipline to find appropriate methodologies with which to address these questions of racial difference, exclusion and silence anew.

Psychoanalytic theory and race

Frantz Fanon, psychoanalyst and cultural theorist, was amongst the first to apply psychoanalysis to the discourses of the colonial gaze and race relations in his 1952 book *Black Skin, White Masks*. Key to his interest in using psychoanalytic models is his desire to tease out the effects of colonial rule and racial oppression on the Black psyche. Adopting this methodological approach rooted in his own post-colonial experience (he was born on the French Caribbean island of Martinique) allows him to render the very category of race suspect; for the Black person, he argues, only experiences psychological problems when they come to be perceived by the white coloniser: 'It is the racist who creates his inferior' (1986: 93); 'As long as the Black man is among his own, he will have no occasion, except in minor conflicts, to experience his being through others' (1986: 109). Produced in the imperialist encounter with white racism is a way of knowing race based on the gaze and looking structures, fantasy and terror, cultural taboo and social violations.

Fanon viewed racism and its gazing structures as deeply rooted within the Imaginary. Understanding Lacan's theory of the mirror stage, with its importance of looking in constituting the ego (see, chapter one), gave him the framework to suggest how the Black male (rather than female) body emerges as a site of hysteria around body image, sexuality, masculine identity and racial otherness. The child finds a pleasurable sense of completeness in identifying with the idealised image he assumes to be his own in the mirror. Compensating for the experienced lack, the image of the Other is internalised by the child as the idealised ego and used to mask the terror associated with castration. Yet the visual otherness offered by the Black body leads to what Fanon terms 'Negrophobia' within the colonial imaginary. Representing the real 'possibility of *another* body' (Doane 1991: 25), the Black male body makes visible an imagined sexual completeness for the white man. This in turn means the Black male body cannot be imagined beyond his corporeality and sexual potency. He *is* 'genital', 'perceived on the level of the body image, absolutely as the not-self ... the unidentifiable, the unassimilable' (1986: 161). This perceived hypersexuality of the Black man cannot entirely be separated out from the obvious visibility associated with skin colour. Fetishising skin colour emerges as a neurosis born of the original psychic trauma linked to castration anxiety. For Fanon, the psychic structures of racism intimately equates skin colour with the sexualisation of the Black male body in the colonialist imagination.

Understanding psychological structures that perpetuate racial Otherness is further explored in the work of Homi K. Bhabha. His intervention moved on the debate about the racial Other, to propose that colonial power is discursive and identities for colonial/post-colonial subjects are constructed within discourse. Extending Edward Said's pioneering *Orientalism*,[1] he places attention on 'the *processes of subjectification* made possible (and plausible) through stereotypical discourse' (1992: 313). Drawing also on Michel Foucault's notion of discourse[2] as well as psychoanalytic theory, Bhabha is concerned to locate how the racialised Other is constituted in and maintained through the colonial imagination. 'The construction of the colonial subject in discourse, and the exercise of colonial power through discourse, demands an articulation of forms of difference – racial and sexual' (ibid.). For him, colonialism is an effect of power that turns the problem of racial origin into a tool of colonial administration and juridical authority.

Stereotyping emerges as a strategy by which colonial powers can establish and sustain the right to rule:

> The objective of colonial discourse is to construe the colonised as
> a population of degenerate types on the basis of racial origin, in
> order to justify conquest and to establish systems of administration
> and instruction. (1992: 316)

Stereotyping functions to normalise an image of the Other. This is achieved by initiating knowledge that oscillates between what is already known and somehow fixed, and something which must be anxiously and compulsively replicated in order to maintain credibility.

Bhahba contends that stereotyping is a form of phobic behaviour and the stereotype a type of fetish. He points to the way in which colonial discourse makes visible 'the traumatic impact of the return of the oppressed' through 'those terrifying stereotypes of savagery, cannibalism, lust and anarchy which are the signal points of identification and alienation, scene of fear and desire in colonial texts (1992: 318). These images function like the Freudian fetish, recognising racial, cultural and historical difference and its disavowal:

> What is this theory of encapsulation or fixation which moves between the recognition of cultural and racial difference and its disavowal, by affixing the unfamiliar to something established, in a form that is repetitious and vacillates between delight and fear? Does the Freudian fable of fetishism (and disavowal) circulate within the discourse of colonial power requiring the articulation of modes of differentiation – sexual and racial – as well as different modes of discourse – psychoanalytic and historical? (1992: 319)

Like other forms of fantasy identified by Freud, imagining the racial Other is predicated on the gaze and looking relations. Colonial power involves, argues Bhabha, disciplinary regimes of surveillance over the colonised race. He equates these mechanisms for imperialist gazing with Freudian theories around looking – voyeurism and scopic drives. 'I suggest that in order to conceive of the colonial subject as the effect of power that is productive – disciplinary and "pleasurable" – one has to see the *surveillance* of colonial power as functioning in relation to the regime of the *scopic* drive' (1992: 322).

These psychoanalytic-inspired studies that explored how imperial gazing and colonial surveillance function to enclose the racial subject within a complex nexus of power/knowledge provided a starting point for feminist scholars like Mary Ann Doane. She suggests that the Black male as Other 'would appear analogous to that of the woman in psychoanalysis, who embodies castration' (1991: 225). Whereas the woman as lack represents the threat of castration for the white male, the threat associated with the Black man relates to his '*overpresence*, [his] monstrous penis' (ibid.). Analysing how *Birth of a Nation* (D. W. Griffith, 1915) uses melodramatic codes, textual patterns and cross-editing through the theoretical perspectives outined above allows her to identify how the male (imperialist) gaze works. The Black man embodying sexual potency and 'biological danger' and the white woman signifying racial purity justifies the constant surveillance of both, leading either to punishment (the Black man *must* be lynched for desiring the white woman) or protection (the white woman/nation *must* be saved from miscegenation).Yet the woman defined here is white, leading Doane to claim that, 'there is a sense in which it is strongly applicable to Black women, who are the objects of a double surveillance linked to race and gender' (1991: 223). The attempt to address the theoretical lack around the Black woman and her historical silence prompted feminists to rethink the engagement between psychoanalysis and race.

Rethinking psychoanalysis, feminist film theory and the Black woman

The theoretical impasse between psychoanalytic theory and representations of the Black woman in history is interrogated in the work of Jane Gaines. Her study laid the foundation for discussions around the gaze and 'white' privilege within feminist film theory, with its investigation into the power of looking relations and Black female sexuality. She starts by first identifying the limits of 'the psychoanalytic concept of sexual difference' for it 'is unequipped to deal with a film which is about racial difference and sexuality' (2000: 336). Focusing on the Diana Ross star vehicle *Mahogany* (Berry Gordy, 1975) about an aspiring Black model, Tracy Chambers, reveals to Gaines how this mainstream American movie presents Ross' body as fetish. Long drawn-out fashion shoots, using close-ups and freeze-frames, confirm the Mulvey thesis of how the female body quite literally halts narrative flow. But, argues Gaines, white male aggression toward the Black woman (the violent treatment experienced by Tracy at the hands of photographer Sean McEvoy, played by Anthony Perkins) becomes almost lost in the other exploitative gender relationships with which the film deals – the photographer taking advantage of his model, the deranged man violating the model, the voyeur attempting to murder the object of his desire. Eliding questions of race and class oppression around the spectacle of Chambers/Ross within the film's unconscious ideological signifying practices seems to be symptomatic of the broader cultural difficulties in representing Black femaleness: 'The psychoanalytic model works to block out considerations which assume a different configuration, so that, for instance, the Freudian-Lacanian scenario can eclipse the scenario of race-gender relation in Afro-American history, since the two accounts of sexuality are fundamentally incongruous' (2000: 337).

Possessing the Black female body in the gaze is a white male privilege. Key to understanding the right to look, argues Gaines, is not 'psychoanalytic categories' (2000: 346) but specific socio-cultural historical discourses on American slavery and race relations. Slavery, for example, gave white masters license to openly look at Black slaves while Blacks were prohibited from the gaze. Turning to history and African-American literature challenges dominate white feminist notions about the construction of male visual pleasures, suggesting instead how acts of looking are grounded in specific socio-cultural historical discourses defined by power, subjugation, oppression and myth.

Historical considerations underpin representations of Black female sexuality. Gaines explores how contemporary Black feminist criticism identifies the body of the Black female subject as a site of cultural resistance. She represents the 'paradox of a non-being' (Hortense Spillers, quoted in Gaines 2000: 351), referring back to a time in American history when the Black woman as a historical subject did not exist: a period when she was "designated as not human" (ibid.) and her body did not belong to her. Out of this socio-cultural historical discourse, Black female sexuality is defined as excess, 'as unfathomable and uncodified' (ibid.) within mainstream American cinema. Gaines takes this reasoning further, to suggest that the 'apparent elusiveness' may be because the Black woman cannot be explained by the methodologies currently used by feminism. Models defined by orthodox psychoanalytic paradigms and patriarchal power in fact seem incapable either of making sense of, or speaking for, the Black woman. She calls on feminist film theory to move beyond the '"universalist tendency" found in both Freud and Lacan' (2000: 352); and insists that it is imperative feminism ask different questions and find more appropriate methodologies to 'comprehend the category of the real historical subject' (2000: 352).

Claire Pajaczkowska and Lola Young, responding to Fanon's challenge for a psychoanalytic understanding of racism that interrogates 'Negrophobia' and help promote understanding of an autonomous Black culture, contribute another perspective for feminism. Identifying first how psychoanalysis was conceived by 'Jewish survivors of persecution and diaspora' (2000: 356), the authors understand the discourse as being about deconstructing oppression – who oppresses who, and how individuals work through acts of oppression. For them, 'a psychoanalytic perspective makes it possible to draw on intuition, experience and memory in a critical account of racism' (2000: 357). Detailing a number of psychoanalytic concepts – trauma, the unconscious, identification, denial and the Oedipus complex – allows these scholars to account for an imperialist rationale established by the white man to justify the brutal treatment of indigenous peoples under their control:

> The emotional flow is from anxiety to denial to projection: then to distortion upon which enactment is based and from there, there is further denial. This cycle is important politically because the enactment phase involves the mechanics of individual, institutional and state racisms. (2000: 369)

White colonial power determines the realities of indigenous populations through a series of projections that oppress individual groups and repress non-white cultures in order to mask racial anxieties.

Pajaczkowska's inquiry into Neil Jordan's 1986 film *Mona Lisa* explores how the sexuality of the Black woman, Simone (Cathy Tyson) emerges as something that must be 'investigated, controlled [and] possessed' (2000: 364). Exposing her activities as a prostitute leads the central male protagonist (the white working-class George, played by Bob Hoskins) to commit acts of voyeurism, violence involving guns and parricide, before Simone is finally repressed by the narrative and disappears. Young's study of Toni Morrison's novel *Beloved* (1987) offers a different perspective of the Black female subject in relation to acts of disavowal and repression, to suggest that the narrative explores 'remembering and speaking the unspeakable past as a means of understanding and progressing forward from the often overwhelming present' (2000: 365). The psychoanalytic notion of the 'talking cure' is used here not only to understand how film and literary texts deal with remembering the trauma of slavery and the resulting fragmented sense of cultural identity for the Black woman but also by Young in particular to understand her own repressed memories through identification. Making known traumatic acts of historical persecution and personal repression results in Young being able to think about how the Black female subject/reader could possibly reclaim cultural self-identity, experience and memories from 'historical amnesia and national disavowal' (2000: 372). She insists that we must endeavour to journey further into 'the interior of the "dark continent"' (2000: 373).

Colonial imaginings, discourses on 'race' and representing the Black woman as spectacle

Young denounces the way in which orthodox feminism has relied too heavily on Freud's 'dark continent' metaphor to describe white European female sexuality as unknowable to men. So much so that the 'racial and colonial implications' had all but been eliminated (1996: 177). Two scholars offer an important corrective in this regard: Ella Shohat and Mary Ann Doane. Shohat stresses how discourses on race and racism are deeply embedded in Freud's accounts of analysing and 'knowing' female sexuality:

> [The] process of exposing the female Other, of literally denuding her ... comes to allegorise the Western masculine power of possession ... she, as a metaphor for her land, becomes available for Western penetration and knowledge. This intersection of the epistemological and the sexual in colonial discourse echoes Freud's metaphor of the 'dark continent'. Freud speaks of female sexuality in metaphors of darkness and obscurity often drawn from the realms of archaeology and exploration – the metaphor of the 'dark continent', for example, deriving from a book by the Victorian explorer Stanley. Seeing himself as explorer and discoverer of new worlds, Freud ... compared the role of the psychoanalyst to that of the archaeologist 'clearing away the pathogenic psychical material layer by layer' which is analogous 'with the technique of excavating a buried city'. (1991: 57)

Making known the rules that operate within Freud's 'dark continent' metaphor – the impossibility of the man knowing the woman – allows Shohat to put forward a persuasive case for arguing that his assumptions and expectations about the Otherness of female sexuality are rooted in colonial ways of thinking about race and power. Although her work does not go far enough to question the absent Black woman, it does offer insight into how Freud's Id/Superego dichotomy parallels the primitive/civilised binary, in which the constitution of the (white) male ego is predicated upon the denial of women and peoples categorised as primitive while establishing an important link between colonialism, psychoanalysis and cinema (Doane 1991; Kaplan 1993).

Doane contends that the 'dark continent' metaphor can help scholars understand the complex 'historical articulation of the categories of racial difference and sexual difference' (1991: 212). She points in particular to how nineteenth-century literature and visual culture produced by the colonial imagination persistently equated the African woman with the African continent – 'the conquest of the former signified the successful appropriation of the latter' (1991: 213). Photographic images brought back from the 'dark continent' mapped exotic/erotic locations onto the body of the native women. Doane cites in particular Sander L. Gilman's (1985) findings on how the Black woman became incommensurable with a primitive, promiscuous sexuality in the popular nineteenth-century European imagination. He demonstrates how the female Hottentot (Khosian people from South Africa) embodied fecundity and an excessive sexuality, becoming an icon of Black female sexuality for over a century. First exhibited for public amusement, the Hottentot Venus (a young Khosian woman named Saarjite Baartman brought to Britain in 1810 and displayed naked for a paying audience) soon became an object of Imperialist scientific research. Medical dissection, wax models of her genitalia and pseudo-scientific treatises made her sexuality known. Her steatopygia (enlarged buttocks) and 'distended labia' constituted a pathology of the Black woman, which in turn translated her into a powerful representation of primitive hypersexuality and racial inferiority. Social, political, scientific and philosophical assumptions of the hyperbolically sexual African woman, and reinforced by colonial relations, were used by white men to justify their treatment of Black women (either taken as concubines or sold as prostitutes). Her conclusion is that feminists must identify the historical ways of knowing race and sexual difference in order to start exposing how racial and sexual ideologies construct representational typologies and ways of seeing.

Lola Young works through the implications of Shohat and Doane's arguments, to offer an inter-disciplinary approach to studying the 'conjunction of race, gender and sexuality in British cinema' (1996: 1). Central to her thinking is how cinematic images of race and gender are related to ways of 'knowing' racial and sexual difference rooted in Britain's colonial past:

Cultural production, the dissemination of historical information and the pursuit of knowledge in western Europe should be understood and analysed within a framework which recognises the centrality of racial difference in the construction of colonial and post-colonial black and white identities. (1996: 188)

Racial categories were taken as a way of defining and locating Britain's Others, which in turn enabled the colonialist to economically exploit 'their' overseas territories and justify the right to do so. Just as Mulvey understood the power relations involved in the gaze and visual pleasures, Young racialises her thesis, to suggest how the cinema as an instrument of power, subjugation and control of the racial Other coincided with a period of imperial expansion in search of new markets.

Of particular interest to Young is how those socio-cultural and historical anxieties commensurate with identities and borders are mapped onto the body of the Black woman. It is a process that turns her into an uneasy image of hyperbolic sexuality and object of racial suspension requiring constant surveillance. Increasingly the Black female body became subject to scientific investigation and medical inquiry. Elaborate and detailed examinations of the Black body were carried out in a context in which the supremacy and importance of what white Europeans had to say went unquestioned. Such thinking fed into British cinema, whereby Black women became inhibitors of male (narrative) progression. Either these women chose 'material wealth and social prestige' over political activism such as in *Pressure* (Horace Ove, 1974) and *Black Joy* (Anthony Simmons, 1977), or become associated with a perverse and 'primal' sexuality as in *Leo the Last* (John Boorman, 1969) and *Mona Lisa* (Neil Jordan, 1986). They are depicted as 'victims, purveyors of transgressive sexuality or emblematic silent bystanders, and as politically naïve and assimilationist' (1996: 180). What is at stake in these films is not an active Black female subjectivity but 'competing masculinities' (ibid.), in which the woman of colour emerges as the site where this gendered conflict is played out. For Young, it is important for the academy 'to address the ways in which questions of ethnicity and racial difference are structured into texts and their analyses' (1996: 181).

Imperial gazing, inter-racial looking relations and the oppositional gaze

Questions raised by Young about how the colonial gaze becomes sexualised when trained on the Black woman, as well as who has the right to look and define the Other, are issues addressed by E. Ann Kaplan in *Looking for the Other: Feminism, Film and the Imperial Gaze*. Looking relations, as Kaplan understands it, are determined by power and knowledge, inseparable from how subjectivities are constituted, and from historical and cultural specificities. Drawing on theories of nation, race and psychoanalysis, she argues that ways of seeing and inter-racial looking are deeply ingrained in Western imperialism; and hinge on arguments that circulated around ideas of national identity, cultural stereotypes and racial origins, in which the supremacy and importance of European (and later American) civilisation went unquestioned. Looking at 1930s Hollywood films like *King Kong* (Merian C. Cooper, 1933) and *Tarzan, the Ape Man* (W. S. Van Dyke, 1932) reveals to her how the male cinematic gaze and the colonial gaze are linked. Travelling to 'dark continents' finds the male protagonist controlling and mastering land, natives and women through his gaze. Whereas the white male looks at the white woman or Black man (possibly looking at a Black woman as in *King Kong* when white men look on as the Indonesian men sacrifice a young native woman to the giant gorilla), there is no one looking back at the white man.

Interrogating ways of knowing which shape representation and produce forms of inter-racial looking sets the agenda for Kaplan's theoretical project. She attempts to think about 'what happens when modernist subject-object looking structures are replaced by new, postmodernist ones, generated by a different set of technologies and by new global flows of bodies, money, ideas and media?' (1997: 12). Examining inter-racial looking relations and its implications for film feminism, she focuses on contemporary women filmmakers like Julie Dash, Claire Denis, Pratibha Parmar, Gurinder Chadha and Trinh T. Minh-ha to examine how they are 'producing new ways of seeing, new readings of the past, as well as new images of inter-racial looking relations' – to look differently beyond the constraints of Western thinking and the oppressive colonial gaze, and 'change how images are produced' in the process (1997: 219).

Asian British women filmmakers, for example, have explored subject-ivities-in-between and inter-racial looking relations while delving into the difficulties of being accepted as British. Deconstructing Chadha's 1993 film *Bhaji on the Beach* leads Kaplan to note how the film resists the repressive imperialist gaze to look differently. What intrigues her most is how the film reverses the gaze – the look is firmly located from within the Indian diaspora community living in the English Midlands. A typical scene revealing how inter-racial looking relations work is one in which the Asian women, travelling to Blackpool for a day at the seaside, encounter a group of white working-class men. Punished for rebuffing their crude advances, the women are subjected to jeering insults and loutish behaviour. That the white male gaze turns so quickly from lust to violence reveals misogyny in their virulent racism. Not content with verbal abuse, the men expose themselves to the women as the van overtakes the bus the women are in. Differences amongst the women related to age, religious propriety, links to traditional Indian culture, or a sense of belonging to Britain are revealed in the various reactions, for while the older women are mortified, others are distressed, and others find it merely funny. Seen from the eyes of the Asian women positions the spectator not only to share the shock, pain and eventual laughter with the women, but also to experience the sadistic racism of the white male gaze in its right to look.

Kaplan turns to Lyotard's notion of the *différend* – meaning an un-resolvable difference between two parties because no rules that apply to both sides can be established (Lyotard 1988: 5) – to tackle the complex issue of 'knowing the Other' and 'the ambivalence of the colonial relation' (Kaplan 1997: 155). Deconstructing complex historical contexts and analysing subjectivities formed through the imperial gaze offer 'a different way of thinking through and imagining problems of nation, global relations, imperialism' (1997: 179–80).

Hybrid identities

E. Ann Kaplan's work on seeing differently is related to the recent cross-cultural feminist efforts aimed at theorising the hybrid subject and the diaspora 'in-between' experience. Such a discussion is embedded in and shaped by postmodern and post-colonial thinking, in which questions of fragmented, or hybrid, subject-identities are central. Research undertaken by Arjun Apparduria (1993) and Paul Gilroy (1993) theorise the dislocation felt by diasporic peoples of colour. Crucial to this debate is the difficulty of conceiving the speaking racial subject beyond traditional power/know-ledge paradigms. Gayatri Chakravorty Spivak summarises the problem of speaking from *outside* the hegemony of Western imperialist thinking:

> I am thinking basically about the imperialist project which had to assume that the earth that it territorialised was in fact previously

uninscribed. So then a world, on a simple level of cartography, inscribed what was assumed to be uninscribed. Now this worlding is also a texting, textualising, a making into art, a making into the object to be understood. (1990: 1)

Establishing adequate theoretical frameworks and forms of representation to convey an authentic subject-identity is now firmly on the agenda.

British-Asian independent filmmaker and feminist critic, Pratibha Parmar, shares this interest in the 'myths, fictions and fantasies which have in turn shaped the nature of encounters between contemporary Black and migrant settlers and the predominantly white populace of the metropolis' (1990: 115). But her films and critical work seek to move beyond deeply ingrained fantasies about, and the institutionalised ways of knowing, the ethnic Other to rethink race, gender and looking relations anew. Her 1991 film *Khush* combines documentary forms with fantasy sequences to give representation to Asian lesbian and gays living in India and as part of the diaspora. 'One recurring sequence involves two Indian women in an intimate setting watching an old Bollywood movie. Rather than fragmenting body parts into fetish (common to commercial cinema), the female body is filmed in total – presented for the camera as complete. In this way, the film attempts to take back the ground purloined by the mainstream – to enter boldly into that terrain of filming the female body, but doing it in her very different way, with her different eye' (Kaplan 1997: 285).

Asserting an intimate relationship between the theoretical, aesthetic concerns and personal experience encourages Parmar to begin 'recoding ... with our diasporan sensibilities' (2000: 376). Of what this collective project means to women of colour like herself, she writes '[our] ancestral as well as personal experiences of migration, dispersal and dislocation give us an acute sense of the limitations of national identities' (ibid.). Her work is less about understanding than resisting marginalisation, to conceive of 'a new politics of difference (2000; 377):

We are creating a sense of ourselves and our place within different and sometimes contradictory communities, not simply in relation to ... not in opposition to ... nor in reversal to ... nor as a corrective to ... but in and for ourselves. Precisely because of our lived experiences of racism and homophobia, we locate ourselves not within any one

community but in the spaces between these different communities
... images that evoke passionate stirrings and that enable us to
construct ourselves in our complexities. (2000: 377–8)

Use of present tense and first-person voice defines her work here. It gives
her theoretical model a contemporaneousness as well as a sense of
process being made visible – a theory about a process of becoming.

For Trinh T. Minh-ha, knowing the ethnic Other is 'to reopen endlessly
the fundamental issue of science and art; documentary and fiction;
universal and personal; objectivity and subjectivity; masculine and
feminine; outside and inside' (1991: 65). Coming from the diasporic
intellectual position as a Vietnamese living in America, she alerts us to
the problems involved in locating an authentic voice for the Other since
all subjectivities are created in discourse and shaped by discursive power
and knowledge. The truth of experience cannot simply be communicated;
rather it is discourse itself within which truth comes into being that must
be interrogated:

I am in the midst of a knowing, acquiring, deploying world
– I appropriate, own and demarcate my sovereign territory as I
advance – while the 'other' remains in the sphere of acquisition.
Truth is the instrument of a mastery which I exert over areas of the
unknown as I gather them within the field of the known. (1991: 12)

Defining the Other is essential to the maintenance of the master discourse,
for the marginality of the Other confirms the power of the centre and its
right to rule. Allowing the native insider to bear witness to his/her own
cultural heritage and environment means that the master (white) discourse
can authenticate knowledge it feels unqualified to speak about. With that
said, the master discourse only makes known what it wants to hear and
see: 'We have to train Insiders so that they may busy themselves with Our
preoccupations, and make themselves useful by asking the right kind of
Question and providing the right kind of Answer' (1991: 68).

In her films, photographs, music and theoretical writings, Trinh
struggles with the question of how to define oneself as 'subject', both as
an individual and in relation to women from different cultural and national
contexts. Combining theory with practice like Pramar, her pioneering
work is deeply embedded in the postmodern and post-colonial projects

on the complexities of subject formation and how subject-identities are always in the process of becoming. For this post-colonial, feminist filmmaker the subject formed through the experience of being at and crossing over borders – of official white culture, of patriarchal thinking, of geographical frontiers and colonial territories – challenges the legitimacy of the dominant discourse to speak about and define the Other. This new kind of subject makes visible unease in the way their existence blurs and constantly disrupts the strict me/Other, subject/object binaries that keeps Western knowledge intact, for it is these demarcations within which Western thought comes to know the world and maintains its right to rule. At the colonial periphery and from the patriarchal margins, different rules and non-totalising strategies exist 'to suspend meaning and resist closure' (1991: 74), and prevent the ruling centre from definitively categorising 'according to its own ethnocentric classifications' (1991: 17). Both as a filmmaker and theoretician, Trinh seeks to agitate, contest, reverse and displace seemingly assured Western hegemonic positions that 'naturalise a dominant, hierarchically unified worldview' (1992: 207). In the process of 'tracking down and exposing the Voice of power and Censorship whenever and in whichever side it appears' (1991: 73), her work questions the very idea of identity and the speaking 'I'.

For Trinh, woman must negotiate a subject-identity for herself that cannot be named (patriarchy has no language for it) and has already too many names (she is Other). Woman narrates her displacement, calling into question ways of Western thinking and contesting the subject-object relation:

> She refuses to reduce herself to an Other and her reflections to a mere outsider's objective reasoning or insider's subjective feeling. She knows ... that she is not an outsider like the foreign outsider. She knows she is different while at the same time being Him. Not quite the Same, not quite the Other, she stands in that undetermined threshold place where she constantly drifts in and out. Undercutting the inside/outside opposition, her intervention is necessarily that of both a deceptive insider and a deceptive outsider. She is this Inappropriate Other/Same who moves about with always at least two/four gestures: that of affirming 'I am like you' while persisting in her difference; and that of reminding 'I am different' while unsettling every definition of otherness arrived at. (1991: 74)

Emerging as the 'Inappropriate Other' herself, and writing such a position into her work, Trinh T. Minh-ha, as a filmmaker and critical thinker, interrogates the truthfulness of Western assumptions in relation to race and gender identity. Questioning what is taken for granted in Western scholarship and science allows her to reveal that, 'the criterion of authenticity no longer proves pertinent' (1991: 76).

Identifying 'displacement' as being about an 'impossible, truthful story of living in-between regiments of truth' (1991: 21), and constantly defying attempts made by the master discourse to define the world, leads Trinh to conclude that a new kind of subjectivity is produced by and within this process. It is a subjectivity always constituting itself from a multiple of identities, truths and voices, separate but interdependent, which defies easy classification within conventional categories of race, gender and national identity. This 'subject-in-process' (1991: 48) speaking her plurality, formed across generations, cultures and geographical spaces, 'never freed from historical and socio-political contexts nor entirely subjected to them', reveals subjectivity to be inherently unstable and constantly at risk from 'being no-thing' (1991: 48). Developing her thinking here enables her to identify a new type of criticism where one does not 'speak about' but instead 'speaking nearby' (1992). It is a way of talking that does not take possession or pretend to know the other. Rather 'speaking nearby' recognises the gap between people. The phrase conveys an idea of closeness while retaining the necessary distance created by difference; it is a concept of 'approaching' rather than 'knowing' the other.

Reassemblage (1986) plays with the conventions of the ethnographic documentary to locate new ways of knowing and speaking about a culture beyond another. Inspired by her visit to West Africa where she was teaching and studying music in Senegal, her film attempts to locate a position from which to speak in a culture that is not her own. Avoiding single narrative or spectatorship positions, she instead creates and juxtaposes numerous voices and desperate images. Kaplan explains:

> There is a deliberate disjunction of sound and image; there is the sudden cutting off of sound while the image continues; there are repetitions of sounds and images in different parts of the film that do not necessarily connect; there are surprising images (the sudden appearance of the albino children; the sudden appearance of a Western plastic doll – a trace, perhaps, of the anthropologist

or tourist who is absent; the gruesome recurring shots of the dead animal...). None of this is explained. The spectator must find a way to do something with it on her own – which is precisely the challenge that Trinh sets in order to unsettle spectator's normal viewing processes. (1997: 202)

Of importance to Trinh T. Minh-ha is how 'to make a film in which the viewer – where visually present or not – is inscribed in the way the film is scripted and shot ... Through a number of creative strategies, this process is made visible and audible to the audience who is thus solicited to interact and to retrace it in viewing the film' (2000: 334). Trinh demands the audience construct '"their own film" from the film they have seen' (2000: 335), to create new meanings and experiences for the film beyond what the filmmaker may have intended.

Literary criticism, autobiographical writings and 're-memory'

Recent film analysis conceived by Black feminists turns to a longer tradition of Black literary criticism (Smith 1977a, 1977b; Christian 1985, 1989), and Black creative writing projects (Walker 1983, 1984, 1989; Lorde 1982, 1984, 1988). Looking to the reservoir of ideas, storytelling forms and conceptual thinking produced in literary critiques and writing styles gives Black feminist film analysis alternative tools to open out the question of Black female subjectivity anew in terms of spectatorship (Bobo 1995; Wallace 1993, 1997), and representation. Such work aims to put right the misrepresentation, historical silence and absence of Black women in mainstream cultural forms; and to identify radical forms of representation and narrative that allow Black women to tell their stories differently.

It is a theoretical approach firmly rooted in cultural practice, both visual and literary. bell hooks (1992) in particular demands that film theory enter into dialogue with Black history and creativity. It is a dialogue that turns to newly invented and/or concealed stories in order to reveal alternative representational types and ways of speaking about experience. Other enunciation processes shaped by family histories and first-person female narrators (diaries, letters), and/or located in non-European white cultural storytelling traditions, including polyrhythmic structures, call and response (or antiphony) and folk tales, prove integral to the process. Black feminist filmmakers/writers and scholars are actively engaged in creating an alternative representational system and ways of speaking. It is a point noted by Barbara Christian (1989) who contends that Black women are only silenced and defined as minority by the logic of white academic practices and theory. The task ahead for women of colour is to theorise race and gender using forms – or what she calls 'hieroglyphs' – that are different from those defined by Western hegemony. Autobiographical techniques and criticism that recognise the speaker aim to challenge the neutrality of Western logic.

Integrating the writing of theory with practical approaches to creating new images and narrative forms is a key feature of this intervention. Just as Trinh T. Minh-ha and Pratibha Parmar ('I am also interested in making work that documents our stories and celebrates and validates our existence to ourselves and our communities' (2000: 378)) write theory into their films about hybrid identities and the enunciation of 'I' (as noted above), Alice Walker and André Lorde find narrative forms that allow the Black subject to tell her story set apart from restrictive patriarchal interpretations:

> This work aims to highlight the mobility of Black culture and to deconstruct the fixed binaries of white culture, a particularly important theme when diasporic cultures owe much to colonial pressures. (Humm 1997: 120)

What we are witnessing then is a new repertoire of images and stories about non-white women emerging.

Hazel Carby (1987) identifies how Black women's cultural forms produce a 'usable past'. She contends that the quest to find a usable past is partly inspired by the diasporic experience – to locate identities and speak of experience beyond restrictive white hegemonic interpretations. Furthermore this quest is always constituted in the writing of the narrative or film diegesis. Christian considers a similar process at work in what she terms as 're-memory.' She seeks to understand a Black feminist aesthetics as being about a dialogue between 'ordinary' Black women and their female ancestors. Utilising the tools made available by Black feminist creative writing, Julie Dash is able to challenge dominant codes of filmmaking in her film *Daughters of the Dust* (1990) – a film set in 1902 that chronicles the lives three generations of Gullah women from the Peazant family over two-days. Structured around Ibo's migration from the Sea Islands off the South Carolina coast to mainland America and Nana

Peazant's remembering stories from Africa, it refigures a moment in Gullah history. Such a historical moment is embodied in and through the Gullah women – female conversations, the local vernacular, oral traditions, female kinship relations, the memories of Nana Peazant, and cultural products produced by the women (like Nana's family tree made of bottles). These narrative and symbolic strategies are conveyed through Dash's subversion of dominant filmmaking techniques, in which she disrupts, recodes and reinvents film conventions. Film texts made by women of colour are producing non-white feminist aesthetics and narrative strategies as well as writing new theories about experience, memory and history in the process of producing representation.

Mimicry, race and racial ambivalence

Colonial mimicry is the desire for a reformed, recognisable Other, as a subject of a difference that is almost the same. Which is to say that the discourse of mimicry is constructed around an ambivalence; in order to be effective, mimicry must continually produce its slippage, its excess, its difference ... Mimicry emerges as the representation of difference that is itself a process of disavowal. Mimicry is thus the sign of a double articulation; a complex strategy of reform, regulation and discipline, which 'appropriates' the Other as it visualises power. Mimicry is also the sign of the inappropriate, however, a difference or strategic function of colonial power, intensifies surveillance, and poses an immanent threat to both 'normalised' knowledges and disciplinary powers ... What they all share is a discursive process by which the excess or slippage produced by the *ambivalence* of mimicry (almost the same, *but not quite*) does not merely 'rupture' the discourse but becomes transformed into an uncertainty which fixes the colonial subject as a 'partial' presence. (Bhabha 1994: 86)

Theoretical interventions into race and looking relations have significantly impacted on the field of feminist film theory, inspiring the discipline to rethink ideas of gender identity and sexual difference in relation to theories on race. Tania Modleski in particular explores mimicry and mimesis in relation to race and sexual difference in mainstream cinema. Her discussion is indebted to Bhabha's thinking (1984, 1992, 1994) about colonial ambivalence and the role played by mimicry in the psycho-social dynamics of colonialism and racism. She understands his use of the term mimicry as involving one nation imposing its institutions, language, socio-cultural values onto the nation it has colonised. Imposition rather than total destruction of the colonialised culture reveals to Bhabha an essential ambivalence within the colonialist project, involving a desire for 'difference that is almost the same' (1994: 131).

Black mimicry of white cultural values emerges as an ambivalent strategy to interrogate and deconstruct racial segregation and cultural attitudes. Studying Whoopi Goldberg allows Modleski to investigate how Goldberg signifies a kind of gender trouble in which 'gender, anatomy and performance are at odds with one another' (1991: 132). In *Ghost* (Jerry Zucker, 1990) she plays the medium Oda Mae Brown who stands in (quite literally at the end) for the dead white male, Sam (Patrick Swayze). Despite its appearance, her body, which allows the lovers to be reunited, disrupts the white heterosexual romance as the norm. *Jumpin' Jack Flash* (Penny Marshall, 1986) and *Fatal Beauty* (Tom Holland, 1987) find her dressing up in high fashion, in which humour arises from her presenting herself as 'in Bhabha's word's, "not-quite a woman" ... Goldberg's donning of women's clothes is seen to be a form of drag – of black female mimicry of (white) femininity, and when she dresses in such clothes she walks in an exaggeratedly awkward fashion like a man unaccustomed to female accoutrements' (ibid.) Such performance of white femininity and heterosexual romance interrupt fantasies in which most Black women will not participate.

Modleski extends her argument to analyse the function of minstrelsy and its practise within the cultural imagination of the coloniser for feminist theory. Turning again to Bhabha's account of the way in which the 'not quite/not white' difference of the colonised person relates to the psychoanalytic concept of fetish allows her to think about how mimicking another race involves the recognition and disavowal of racial differences. Genderising such a process gives her the means to examine further how female mimicry acknowledges 'the vicious circularity of patriarchal thought whereby darkness signifies femininity and femininity darkness? (1994: 120).

A more recent essay in her *Old Wives' Tales* collection explores how female performers appropriate the discredited blackface tradition to explore desire and identity. Reading Sandra Bernhard's cross-racial mimicry in *Without You I'm Nothing* (John Boscovich, 1990) through queer theory and American minstrelsy enables her to think about the ways in which Bernhard uses impersonations of African-American artists as a self-conscious strategy to explore racial identities and lesbian desire anew: 'Assuming blackface allows Sarah to explore her identity along a racial continuum, in which the Jew as outsider stands somewhere between the white Christian and the African American' (1999: 88). Editing and staging patterns position Bernhard as performing for a single white female spectator. The significance of this nameless woman reveals an oscillation around racial masquerade and (white) female desire. For Modleski, this woman signifies 'the white lesbian's desire to desire exogamously and is presented as a kind of fantasised way out of the dilemmas of embodiment … as well as dilemmas of (Jewish and white lesbian) identity' (1999: 93).

Work carried out by scholars like Modleski respond to the demands from Black film feminism to challenge orthodox thinking on looking relations and racial identity, and change the narrative. Interventions around race confront the white feminist academy with its own limitations and acts of oppression. In so doing, debates initiated by those cited above in uttering how racist ideologies produce knowledge opened up new ways of thinking and knowing race and gender as well as exposed the difficulties involved in speaking differently and representing difference. These women put forward more flexible models able of making known the experience of those who possess multiple cultural loyalties, and often endure different types of oppression. Insights provided by theoriests/filmmakers into the unstable nature of identities are groundbreaking. What these theoretical interventions teach us is that we must analyse representation as a site of struggle, and as part of a complex web of competing knowledge.

4   CONCEIVING SUBJECTIVITY, SEXUAL DIFFERENCE AND
     FANTASY DIFFERENTLY: PSYCHOANALYSIS REVISITED
     AND QUEERING THEORY

Long has a dialogue between feminism and psychoanalysis existed. Central to scholarly thinking involving psychoanalysis is the attempt to deconstruct female visual pleasures and identify appropriate models that can adequately account for female subjectivity and desire beyond restrictive binary structures defined by masculine spectatorial pleasures – pre-eminently scopophilia and fetishism. Psychoanalytic film feminism proved central to the formative stages of feminist film theory but has in recent years receded as a methodology. Comparison of these debates is often compromised because film feminism draws on complex theoretical models, many of which are no longer familiar to students. I aim to identify the different feminist arguments by placing them in an intellectual context and unpacking the theoretical methodologies on which they draw.

The ahistoricism and universalism of earlier psychoanalytic film feminism discussed in chapter one proved a starting point for many to renew and extend their critique of psychoanalysis as an appropriate methodological tool for feminist film theory. The influence of New French Feminisms in particular contributed significantly to this project.[1] Feminist scholarship returned to original psychoanalytic writings on, for example, the feminine Oedipal complex to rethink the (unconscious) processes involved in gendered spectatorship (Doane 1987, 2000a, 2000b), as well as revise concepts of subjectivity, sexual difference and fantasy (Rose 1988; Cowie 1997; de Lauretis 1994). Psychoanalysis provided scholars with, in the words of Elizabeth Cowie, 'the most cogent and compelling description and theory of women's sexuality and desire' (1997: 9), and the dialogue helped feminists produce alternative theoretical models to rigorously challenging dichotomies and conceive of subjectivity, sexuality and sexual difference differently.

Into the 1990s and new perspectives were introduced by those involved in queer theory and lesbian/gay studies. Not only did this work aim to remedy theoretical gaps within existing models but also asked different questions. The rise of gay/lesbian studies is an area of scholarly activity made possible by the juxtaposition of social movements such as second-wave feminism and the gay liberation movement alongside theoretical approaches associated with poststructuralism and postmodernity. Increasingly these scholars distanced themselves from the limiting heterosexual binaries of existing psychoanalytic models (Wilton 1995). Recognising homosexual viewing practices and subject positions allowed scholars to re-theorise a more complex, multi-positioned engagement with film. From Teresa de Lauretis' theory of perverse desire (1994) to queer theories pioneered by the likes of Elizabeth Grosz and Judith Butler, this new body of knowledge opened up fresh directions for understanding subjectivity, sexual difference and viewing pleasures.

The riddle of femininity: female sexuality and Freudian thinking revisited

Sigmund Freud begins his 1933 lecture on femininity by noting that women presented psychoanalysis with a dilemma (1986: 412–32). Asking why femininity is psychologically characterised by 'a preference for passive behaviour and passive aims' (1986: 415), he first acknowledges that passivity is defined in part by social customs that 'force women into passive situations' (ibid.). But this only goes some way to solving 'the riddle of femininity' (ibid.). The task ahead for psychoanalysis, he argues, is not to simply 'describe' woman but to set 'about enquiring how she comes into being, how a woman develops out of a child with a bisexual disposition' (1986: 416).

Freud contends that, despite boys and girls sharing similar experiences in the early stages of libidinal development, the female Oedipal trajectory[2] emerges as far 'more difficult and more complicated' (ibid.) than the male equivalent. The reason for this is that she must undertake two additional tasks, explaining further why a girl moves from 'her masculine phase to the feminine one' (1986: 418). Not only does the vagina replace the clitoris as the leading erotogenic zone (a shift from clitoridal masturbation to vaginal intercourse) but also the female child abandons her first love object. Whereas the male child takes his mother as the first love object, a position she holds for the duration of the Oedipal complex, the female child must transfer her affections from the mother to the father. Yet features of this relationship with the father are already established during the pre-Oedipal attachment to the mother. It is important for Freud therefore to understand this earlier phase of female development (and it is this pre-Oedipal development that has intrigued feminists most).

Central to his thinking here on why this strong attachment to the mother ends is the castration complex. On discovering anatomical differences between themselves and the male, the female child, according to Freud, blames her mother for her missing penis and holds her forever responsible for her lack. The female child falls victim to 'penis envy'. Recognising she is without a penis indelibly marks the future development of female subjectivity. Long after she accepts the reality of her lack, her wish 'persists in the unconscious and retains a considerable cathexis [meaning, concentration on a single goal] of energy' (1986: 424). This moment when the female child discovers she is castrated marks a 'turning point' in her formation:

> Three possible lines of development start from it: one leads to sexual inhibition or to neurosis, the second to change of character in the sense of a masculinity complex, the third, finally, to normal femininity. (Ibid.)

The implications of what Freud said about female sexuality: 1) renouncing her phallic sexuality defined by masturbatory pleasure (associated with her now inferior clitoris as well as the mother love-object she holds culpable for her castration); 2) her simultaneous first seeing the penis and immediately understanding the implications which precipitates desire for it; and 3) transferring her desire for a penis onto her attachment to the father – are all issues interrogated and questioned by feminist critical thought and film theory.

A series of female fantasies that also intrigues feminists are the beating fantasies identified by Freud in his 1919 study 'A Child Is Being Beaten' (2001: 179–204). These complex fantasies have three phases and involve a different subject-position each time. The first beating fantasy told by the girl occurs early in her development in which she is watching another child she dislikes being beaten by an adult. Gendered identities of those involved are initially obscure but later it emerges that it is her father administering the thrashing ('My father is beating the child, whom I hate'). The paternal beating of the rival child confirms for the girl that her father loves her. In the next phase the fantasy takes on a decidedly masochistic quality, as the child producing the fantasy is now the one being beaten by the father ('I am being beaten by my father'). Unlike the first fantasy, which is remembered, the second remains unconscious. This transitional form of the fantasy is never remembered by the child but inferred and reconstructed in the analysis. Shame and punishment are now attached to sexual desire, and the incestuous desire of the first fantasy must be repressed and banished to the unconscious. The third phase finds the father translated into an authority figure and the narrator-child no longer figures as a protagonist. Instead the girl, on further questioning by Freud, guesses that, 'I am probably looking on' at another male child (or group of boys) being beaten. '[What] was originally a masochistic (passive) situation is transformed into a sadistic one by means of repression, and its sexual quality is almost effaced' (2001: 199). Such findings lead him to speculate that 'the girl escapes from the demands of the erotic side of her life altogether. She turns herself in fantasy into a man, without herself becoming active in a masculine way, and is no longer anything but a spectator of the event which takes the place of a sexual act' (ibid.). Adopting the position of voyeur results both in the loss of sexual identity and access to her sexuality in relation to the scenario.

Into the 1980s and Freud's account of female-based beating fantasies took on new importance. Revealing the contradictory nature of female fantasies made visible multiple and fluid subject positions, and made it possible to theorise 'a potential split between the sexual object and the sexual aim, between subject and object of desire' (Rose 1988: 210). His explanation of oscillating gender and subject positionings involved in fantasy scenarios helped feminist film theorists locate more open models for understanding female spectatorship, desire and subjectivity. It further enabled them to confront the apparent critical impasse described in Mulvey's thesis with its fixed active/passive, male/female dichotomies.

The desire to desire: Mary Ann Doane, spectatorship and feminine
masquerade

One of the most sustained attempts to reconcile the apparent
contradictions inherent in the psychoanalytic approach to cinema for
feminist film theory is found in the work of Mary Ann Doane. Accepting
the principles laid out by Raymond Bellour, Christian Metz and Laura
Mulvey about the distance between voyeur and screen structured by
psychical mechanisms of voyeurism and fetishism, and identification with
an ego ideal outlined in Lacan's description of the Imaginary (see chapter
one), she notes that previous analyses privilege the male while saying
nothing about the female. Adding to Mulvey's passive/active binary that
of proximity (female) and distance (male) in relation to the image allows
Doane to open up a space for theorising female spectatorship anew. It is
important to understand here that in Doane's work the female spectator
'exists nowhere but *as an effect of discourse*' (1987: 9, my emphasis). Her
theoretical studies explore how the female spectator is 'conceptualised'
within a range of discourses – industrial, institutional and cultural – in
an attempt to move feminist film theory beyond the 'pincers of sexual
difference as binary opposition' (ibid.). Attempting to synthesise the
social and psychical subject of film theory, she is above all interested in
'a certain *representation* of female spectatorship, produced as both image
and position as an effect of certain discourses specified as "belonging" to
the woman' (1987: 8).

To explain nearness, or what she calls the 'claustrophobic closeness'
(2000b: 425), in relation to the female subject, she turns to Freudian
theories and New French Feminisms. Spatial proximity and closeness
to the body are central motifs for the continental feminist philosophers.
Prompted by such thinking, Doane suggests that the female only has to
look at her body to *know* she is castrated (unlike the male who displaces
lack onto the woman and turns her body into fetish).[3] The woman has no
access to such mechanisms of voyeurism and fetishism through which
the male guards himself against castration anxiety. Having no need for
the fetish, for she is already castrated, means the woman is structured
differently within looking relations. Without the prerequisite distancing
mechanisms between self and image, between knowing and seeing in
place (which describes the male experience), the female subject collapses
into the object of her gaze.

Pulling out the implications for a theory of female spectatorship leads Doane to conclude that it is 'proximity rather than distance, passivity, over-involvement and over-identification' which defines the position assigned to the woman in the cinema (1987: 2). Given this over-determined relationship between the female and the image – 'she *is* the image', the female spectator is offered two choices: 'the masochism of over-identification [with the image] or the narcissism entailed in becoming one's own object of desire' (2000b: 433). Suggested here is that the female spectator is forced to identify with herself as image – and one shaped by dominant cultural ideas about femininity. Her image is further commodified and underscored by women's role as consumer: 'she is the subject of a transaction in which her own commodification is ultimately the object' (1987: 30). The female star, along with commodities (fashions, hairstyles) associated with her image, invite the female spectator to consume and be consumed: 'The cinematic image for the woman is both shop window and mirror, the one simply a means of access to the other. The mirror/window takes on then the aspect of a trap whereby her subjectivity becomes synonymous with her objectification' (1987: 33).

A privileged site for analysing 'female spectatorship and the inscription of subjectivity' (1987: 3) is the 'woman's film' from the 1940s, argues Doane. Reasons for favouring these films is because they explicitly acknowledge a female subjectivity, from the female protagonist at the narrative centre to the themes defined as 'female' (domestic concerns, sacrificing personal desires for one's family, and so on), and are grounded in a specific address to an imagined female audience determined by institutional and historical factors. These films were made at a time when Hollywood studios anticipated a predominance of women in the audience (because men were at war), and of seismic social change precipitated by wartime experience that reinscribed gender roles. Taking into consideration these competing forces, she focuses attention on four sub-genres of the 'woman's film' – the 'medical discourse', the maternal melodrama, the love story and the 'paranoid' film.

Given the apparent 'masculinisation' of looking relations in the classical Hollywood cinema, these sub-groupings document a historical crisis in female subjectivity through internal contradictions that allegedly speak about the experience of being female. In fact, argues Doane, '[the] narratives assume a compatibility between the idea of female fantasy and that of persecution – a persecution effected by husband, family or lover'

(1987: 36). Each sub-genre finds the female protagonist masochistically constructed, subject to some kind of patriarchal investigation. Either she is forced to submit her symptomatic body for medical observation and research as in *Dark Victory* (Edmund Goulding, 1939) which finds Judith Traherne (Bette Davis) under medical scrutiny from brain specialist Dr Steele (George Brent); or to gaze in terror upon her own victimisation like in *Gaslight* (George Cukor, 1944) where the more Paula Alquist (Ingrid Bergman) seeks out clues to the mysterious goings-on in her house the more hysterical she becomes. There is an inexorable narrative push, argues Doane, to turn the female protagonist into spectacle: 'The sense of surveillance, of constantly being watched – even as she herself watches – is overwhelming' (1987: 156). This constant surveillance, both inside the narrative and by the cinematic apparatus, complicates female desire and her possession of the gaze. The female protagonist has nothing left but to desire the image of her desire: 'the desire of the woman ... is to duplicate a given image, to engage with and capture the male gaze ... (always situated as a desire to be desired or desirable, hence as subordinate)' (ibid.). She becomes the image of her desires as when Joan Fontaine's character dons a black satin dress she has seen in a fashion magazine to please her husband Maxim de Winter (Laurence Olivier) in *Rebecca* (Alfred Hitchcock, 1940).

Turning to Freud's clinical cases about female beating fantasies described in 'A Child Is Being Beaten' provides Doane with the framework with which to deconstruct the masochistic spectatorial positioning of the females watching these films. What she finds intriguing is the third stage in which the female fantasist supposedly looks upon a (male) child being beaten while attempting to desexualise the fantasy: 'Masochistic fantasy *instead* of sexuality. The phrase would seem to exactly describe the processes in the woman's film whereby the look is de-eroticised" (1987: 19). De-sexualising the gaze, through subjecting the female body to constant surveillance not entirely defined by an erotic gaze (like a medical investigation), disrupts a cinematic address heavily reliant on (masculine) structures of pleasurable looking. Yet in attempting to invalidate the relation between the female body and erotic spectacle described previously by Mulvey, the woman's film places the female spectator in a precarious position. Desexualising the female body problematises female narcissistic identification; and with the film addressing an imagined female audience, and with no active male hero with which to identify, the female spectator finds herself deflected 'away from the ... "transvestite" option ... and toward the more "properly" female identification' (ibid.). Put simply, the female spectator is ushered through the masochistic fantasies of Freud's female Oedipal trajectory toward a passive heterosexual femininity.

Doane's contribution to feminist film theory in rethinking psycho-analytic approaches to female spectatorship is to consider 'the positions from which texts become readable and meaningful to female spectators' (1987: 176) as well as broaden out the debate to ask how female subjectivity is constructed within patriarchal culture. Turning to Michel Foucault's notion of power and knowledge enables her to reconcile these two discussions and expose how '[Western] culture has a quite specific notion of what it is to be a woman and what it is to be a woman looking' (1987: 177). In particular she makes an important connection with what Foucault referred to as 'the fantasy link between knowledge and pain' and the 'association, within patriarchal configurations, of femininity with the pathological' (1987: 38). She exposes 'the all too familiar icons and gestures of femininity' (1987: 37) as being about how the woman's film *produces* discourses of female subjectivity. From the pathological body, suffering either from psychosis or disease, and the desiring women fated to die for love, to the pathos found in the situation where a mother's love for her child reveals the impossibility of female desire, 'we are being subjected to a discourse of femininity' (1987: 181).

One approach that enables Doane to identify a possible subject position for the female spectator as well as to expose femininity as a construct is Joan Riviere's work on female masquerade.[4] Revising Mulvey's transvestite female spectator (in which the woman must imagine herself as male to achieve the required distance from the image to access desire) allows Doane to conclude that the female can stimulate the distance necessary for the pleasure of looking by adopting a feminine masquerade. Quoting Michèle Montrelay she writes, 'the woman uses her own body as a disguise' (2000b: 427). Assuming femininity as a mask to be 'worn or removed', argues Doane, works to destabilise the image and 'confound [the] masculine structure of the look' (ibid.). Masquerade gives the female spectator the opportunity to manufacture a certain distance between herself and the screen image. Rather than collapsing into the film image, the 'feminine' spectator described by Doane is someone able to play with the identities displayed on screen, and tailor them for her own needs and pleasure. Her concept of masquerade both destabilises the female image while confounding masculine structures of the gaze.

Female desire and fantasy

Elizabeth Cowie's 1984 article, 'Fantasia', challenges existing arguments within psychoanalytic film theory and theories of representation. It considers similarities between the types of, and mechanisms involved in, private fantasy of the psychoanalytic subject as well as forms of public fantasy produced by dominant cinema. By reading Freud's papers on public forms of fantasy in 'Creative Writers and Daydreaming', primal fantasies in 'A Case of Paranoia Running Counter to the Psychoanalytic Theory of the Disease' and female fantasies in 'A Child Is Being Beaten' through Jean Laplanche and Jean-Bertrand Pontalis' work on 'Fantasy and the Origins of Sexuality' (1986), Cowie speculates on cinema as a dominant apparatus producing public forms of fantasy, and staging the spectatorial desires through representation.[5]

Laplanche and Pontalis' analysis of seduction fantasy (a reworking of Freud's paper on 'A Child Is Being Beaten') interests Cowie. What intrigues her most is how they characterise the fantasy structure as having 'multiple entries'. Always present in our fantasies means identification is constantly shifting and we are not fixed along lines of sexual difference. Alongside is their characterisation of fantasy as about 'the arranging of, a setting out of, desire; a veritable *mise-en-scène* of desire' (Cowie 1997: 133). The importance placed by Laplanche and Pontalis on the pleasure of fanasy, as being about its *setting* rather than about *having* a desired object, cannot be underestimated: 'Fantasy as a *mise-en-scène* of desire is more a setting out of lack, of what is absent, than a presentation of a having, a being present' (ibid.). Like the original fantasies described by Laplanche and Pontalis through Freud, fantasy scenarios fail to attach the spectator to a specific and polarised gendered position; instead, fantasy scenarios address the spectator in the *staging of desires*.

Starting with Freud's paper on creative writing and daydreaming leads Cowie to view film as being about 'the public circulation of fantasies' (1997: 137). This involves a complex negotiation between social reality, the unconscious and daydreams/conscious wishes. Translating private fantasies into public forms of representation finds the spectator/reader entering into fantasies created by another. Spectators are able to identify with scenarios of desire belonging to someone else 'because fantasy-scenarios involve original wishes which are universal' (that is, seduction fantasies) and because of the various positions structuring the fantasy scenario, 'of loving and/or being loved, of being the father and/or mother, child and/or onlooker' (1997: 140). Film enables us to 'adopt and adapt the ready-made scenarios of fiction, as if their contingent material had been our own' (ibid.).

Now, Voyager (Irving Rapper, 1944) is used by Cowie to illustrate how the film text produces fantasy scenarios. Through a series of transformations undergone by the female lead Charlotte Vale (Bette Davis) – from dowdy spinster to fashionable socialite, from oppressed daughter to adoring surrogate mother – this Hollywood melodrama fulfils a banal series of ambitious and erotic wishes. But this is female Oedipal narrative with a twist. Because Jerry Durrance (Paul Henreid) is married, Charlotte and he cannot be together and their love must remain hidden; instead Charlotte is left to bring up Tina (Janis Wilson), Jerry's daughter, alone. Cowie suggests that 'another (unconscious) scenario of desire' is played out, in which the father is replaced by 'the now good phallic mother' (1997: 149). Her reading reveals 'how the film makes a series of narrative moves between its fantasy scenarios' where pleasure is not bound to the wishes of a single character but instead to how the spectator identifies 'with the playing out of desires' (ibid.). 'This is not Charlotte's fantasy, but the film-text's fantasy. It is an effect of its narration (of its *énonciation*)' (ibid.).

Citing its *énonciation* (meaning, how a film tells its story and to whom) enables Cowie to consider more closely the positions made available for the spectator by the narrative. Cinema as a public form of consuming fantasies involves 'not universal objects of desire, but a setting of desiring in which we can find our place(s)' (1997: 143). Nevertheless, the film narrative 'presumes sexual difference, it presumes the very field of difference which it so relentlessly remakes and it presumes sexual difference in its audience as a condition of its readability, its ability to work for and on its spectators' (1989: 129). Her argument implies an ideological dimension at work in how the narrative organises the fantasy scenarios, and one that endorses spectator positionings defined by sexual difference. While her psychoanalytic account of fantasy makes known the multiple and contradictory positions operating in the film text, and was further extended by Janet Bergstrom (1988) with her looser definition of the multiple identificatory structures at work in the films of Hitchcock, Cowie's work initiates further discussion on the questions of subjectivity, sexual difference and fantasy.

Fantasy theory, psychoanalysis and body genres

Applications of theories on fantasy and psychoanalysis have played a key role in discussions of pornography (Williams 1990), melodrama (Williams 1987: 299–325; Modleski 1999: 31–65) and horror (Creed 1993; Clover 1992). Linda Williams in particular identifies these three genres as marked by 'gratuitous sex, gratuitous violence and terror [and] gratuitous emotion' (1999: 268). Excess of sex, violence and emotion is not only written into the bodies on screen (most notably the sexually saturated female body) but also has physical effects on the body of the spectator linked to original fantasies – seduction and pornography, castration and horror, primal scene and melodrama.

Williams argues that while the spectator is invited to identify with multiple subject positions on screen, the pleasures generated from these fantasies are deeply rooted in cultural preoccupations with gender identities and power relations. For example, a maternal melodrama like *Stella Dallas* (King Vidor, 1937) recognises a 'woman's ambivalent position under patriarchy' (1987: 320) through its multiple, often conflicting, viewing positions which parallels the 'double vision' (1987: 316) experienced by the female spectator: 'The female spectator tends to identify with contradiction itself – with contradictions located at the heart of the socially constructed roles of daughter, wife and mother – rather than with the single person of the mother' (1987: 314). Contradiction can be explained as a 'process of double identification' embedded in a psychoanalytic model of female identity in which girls, as opposed to boys, never lose the intense attachment to the primary love object – the mother – despite turning toward the father. The experience shapes the woman's ability to identify with different subject positions at the same time. Balancing different knowledges and female points of view means the female spectator can see 'the contradictions between what the patriarchal resolution of the film asks us to see – the mother 'in her place' as spectator, abdicating her former position *in* the scene – and what we as empathetic, identifying female spectators can't help but feel – the loss of the mother to the daughter and the daughter to the mother' (1987: 316).

Laplanche and Pontalis' work on structures of fantasy proves useful for Barbara Creed and her work on horror. She notes how the horror genre returns us to the three primal fantasies mentioned above, particularly the origins of sexual difference, while offering fluid identificatory positions across sexual difference and between the extremes of sadism and masochism. Creed considers in particular how horror movies imagine its fantasies of birth, seduction and castration in a *mise-en-scène* defined as abject: 'In these texts, the setting or sequence of images in which the subject is caught up, denotes a desire to encounter the unthinkable, the abject, the other. It is a *mise-en-scène* of desire – in which desire is for the abject' (1993: 154). Moreover the abject – a term borrowed from Julia Kristéva meaning that which does not 'respect borders, positions, rules' and which 'disturbs identity, system, order' (Kristéva 1982: 4) – is more often than not represented by 'the monstrous feminine in one of her guises – witch, vampire, creature, abject mother, castrator, psychotic' (Creed 1993: 154–5). Gender power relations lie at the core of this cultural fantasy, for the monstrous-feminine 'speaks to us more about male fears than about female desire or feminine subjectivity' (1993: 7).

Like Creed, Carol Clover (1992) explores the contemporary horror film to raise questions about the gender politics of mastering the gaze. Drawing on Freud's 'A Child Is Being Beaten' essay and fantasy theory allows her to explain cross-gender identification and gender confusion. Clover reverses the received opinion that violence against women places men in a sadistic role as protagonists and as spectators. She analyses instead how popular slasher films like *The Texas Chainsaw Massacre* (Tobe Hooper, 1974) encourage a masochistic identification, despite the sexual identity of the spectator, with a persecuted final girl pitched against a feminised male killer.

Tania Modleski adopts Freudian theory to explore 'how women find space for their eroticism within the violent structures of patriarchy' (1999: 32) in contemporary melodramas like *The Piano* (Jane Campion, 1993). Exploring the mother/daughter relationship in the film finds her focusing on how '(fantasies of) violence against the mother (as taboo a subject within feminism as outside of it) – becomes crucial to the separation of the daughter from her mother and to the daughter's emergence as a sexual being' (ibid). She charts the shifting narrative position of Flora (Anna Pacquin) from 'being her mother's interpreter to being the mouthpiece of patriarchy' (1999: 42). The daughter's allegiance to her mother changes following Ada's (Holly Hunter) affair with Barnes (Harvey Keitel) and the apparent rebuffal Flora feels. It is a shift marked by Flora's replacement under Ada's hooped skirt (the two camp out under it on the beach) by Barnes.

The exclusion from her mother parallels her sexual awakening. Drawing on Freud's theories of female sexuality and his analyse of girls sadistic play during the phallic phase, Modleski identifies how Flora symbolically gains mastery over her powerlessness at the expense of her mother. Turning away from her mother leads her to bring about her mother's castration – Ada's finger is hacked off by Stewart (Sam Neill) with the words 'I only clipped your wing' – whereby dressed as an angel complete with wings Flora gives the love note meant for Barnes to Ada's husband. Enraged Stewart violently foists the severed digit onto Flora telling her to take it to Barnes. There is nonetheless a happy ending as Barnes takes Ada (and her daughter) to a start a new life away from New Zealand – Ada finds her voice and sexual fulfilment. Most troubling for Modleski though is how the ending negates Flora's traumatic experience: '[The] film draws back from its own bleakness, promoting the mother's story *over* the daughter's and subjecting the latter to a kind of repression' (1999: 46).

Psychoanalysis and the persistence of female homosexuality

As we have seen, psychoanalysis has long struggled with the uneasy question of female subjectivity and desire. In Freud's view, and later revised by Lacan, the female Oedipal journey involves a shift from the girl's active, pre-Oedipal desire for her mother to an acceptance of her castration and transference of desire from mother to father. But, as Freud points out, this 'very circuitous' route toward 'normal' adult femininity is fraught with difficulty. The turning away from the mother in particular proves complicated for the female. Giving up of the exclusive intimacy with, and active libidinal desire for, the mother on discovery of her own castration is never complete. The pre-Oedipal attachment to the mother continues to exert a powerful hold over the female, and thus 'the development of femininity remains exposed to disturbance by the residual phenomena of the early masculine period' (Freud 1986: 429). Put another way, Freud notices that girls are more prone toward bisexuality than boys because of this persistent desire that threatens to pull them back to the mother.

One of the most troubling issues for psychoanalytic theory is the recurring theme of lesbian desire that never quite goes away. Freud argues that this desire is located in the female castration complex. One possible reaction on discovering her castration is 'the development of a powerful masculinity complex' (1986: 427). If the girl refuses to accept her lack, then she defiantly 'clings to her clitoridal activity and takes refuge in an identification with her phallic mother or her father' (1986: 428).

Female homosexuality derives from the disappointment of the female Oedipal love for the father, which in turn drives her 'to regress into her early masculinity complex' (ibid.). Within the Freudian paradigm, the lesbian is defined as either a woman rebelliously refusing to disavow her castration and retaining the female love-object, or one not exhibiting this 'masculine' complex but substituting a phallic woman for the male love-object. Nevertheless, Freud's reading of female homosexuality, as read by Diana Fuss (1993), is about regressing to the pre-Oedipal and primary identification with the mother.

Lesbian desire is no more a possibility for Lacan. Arguing that sexual difference is constituted through language and the Symbolic order, in which the phallic reference governs the sexes, Lacan describes that one either possesses (the male) or embodies (the female) the phallus. If the woman acts as a 'stand-in' for desiring the phallus, then she exists nowhere but as a 'fantasmatic place ... onto which lack is projected, and through which it is simultaneously disavowed' (Rose 1988: 72). Writing on lesbian desire finds Lacan adapting the concept of 'courtly love' (a mediæval courtly practice in which an inaccessible woman becomes the object of desire). Since *only* men can access desire, the lesbian must imagine herself not only as a man in order to desire but also as the object of her own desire. Feminine homosexuality becomes synonymous with a man looking on, or is collapsed into female (heterosexual) desire, 'to be realised in the envy of desire' (Lacan 1982: 97). The lesbian's relation to desire is always inaccessible; and she is left, in the words of Doane, with 'the desire to desire' (1987: 12).

Feminists writing on lesbian subjectivity and desire have for some time focused on the mother/daughter bond as a trope for lesbianism. One of the original papers written on the subject is by Helen Deutsch (1932), in which she views lesbianism as 'a return to the mother'. Julia Kristéva makes a similar connection.[6] She reconsiders the importance of the pre-Oedipal as a utopian feminine space. Drawing heavily on Lacanian psychoanalysis and semiotics, Kristéva identifies the semiotic as a maternal space beyond language and functioning to unsettle the Symbolic . Female homosexuality is imagined as a retreat from the male privileging of the Symbolic into the pre-Oedipal bliss shaped by the symbiotic relationship with the mother. Nancy Chodorow understands lesbian existence as replicating the mother/daughter bonds: because 'the mother remains a primary internal object to the girl ... [lesbian] relationships do tend to re-create mother/daughter emotions and connections, but most women are heterosexual' (1978: 198, 200). Her study of mother/daughter relationship patterns and the female pre-Oedipal simultaneously evokes and writes off lesbianism. Lesbian desire is de-eroticised and located firmly with the realm of the Imaginary/ pre-Oedipal both Kristéva's semiotic and Chodorow's pre-Oedipal.

What these accounts reveal is an 'ignorance and silence about lesbian sexuality' (Wilton 1995: 157–8). Monique Wittig (1992) confirms these difficulties. She contends that lesbians are not women, for she cannot be conceived beyond heterosexuality. Such logic points to the limits of phallocentric discourse to adequately account for the sexual subject, homosexual desire and gender identity outside restrictive hetero-binary paradigms (male/female, queer/straight).

Adrienne Rich sees the failure to make lesbian experience visible, together with the suppression of exclusive female relationships, as rooted in a compulsory heterosexual assumption. What she seeks to understand is how male power works to restrain, and even enforce heterosexuality on, women, concluding that, 'heterosexuality ... needs to be recognised and studied as *a political institution*' (1980: 637). Rich calls on scholars to interrogate the institution of heterosexuality, and introduces two terms – *lesbian existence* and *lesbian continuum* – to break the impasse. The first term refers to reclaiming the fragmented histories and lived experience of real lesbians; and the second relates to critically understanding exclusive female bonding, 'whether we identify ourselves as lesbians or not' (1980: 651). Confronting feminist film theorists and those working in the field of queer theory/lesbian studies is the problem of locating a critical space for discussing representation and spectatorship without recourse to 'the compulsory heterosexuality assumption'. Any attempt to theorise alternative female desire and lesbian subjectivity must first acknowledge the difficulties of finding an appropriate discourse with which to speak of such matters. Silence, loss and exclusion confront scholars, and the task ahead is to make visible the invisible.

(Female) sexuality and its discontents

Kaja Silverman covers familiar ground in her work, to observe that reliance on psychoanalysis by film theorists like Christian Metz and Jean Baudry (1986a; 1986b) results in a film theory obsessed with loss and absence rooted in the trauma of the castration complex. Rethinking these Freudian-based account prompts Silverman to claim that the child is *already* marked by loss long before embarking on the Oedipal journey. Loss begins with the actual separation from the woman's body at birth. This severance from the mother is what Freud describes as 'the prototype of all castration' (1977b: 172).

Starting with Freud's premise that the girl's initial connection with her mother is not pre-Oedipal but the 'negative Oedipus complex' enables Silverman to devise an alternative model of female subjectivity. She turns to Freud's description of two versions of the Oedipal trajectory within which the child must navigate to ensure subjectivity: one works to culturally align the subject with the Symbolic and dominant heterosexual values; while the other 'is culturally disavowed and organises subjectivity in fundamentally "perverse" and homosexual ways' (1985: 120). The first involves identification with the father, and the second references identification with the mother. Recasting Freud means she can relocate maternal identification in the Oedipal realm of loss and absence. Because desire is a product of our entry into the Symbolic, in much the same way as the unconscious is formed as the ego comes into being, the girl's desire for her mother happens *after* her entry into the Symbolic, *after* language and culture is acquired. Such radical reframing allows Silverman to repudiate Kristéva's claim about the de-eroticised mother/child bond consigned to the pre-Oedipal, returning only to disturb the Symbolic. It means that it might at last be 'possible to speak for the first time about a genuinely oppositional desire – to speak about a desire which challenges dominance within representation and meaning, rather than from the place of a mutely resistant biology or sexual essence' (1985: 124).

Silverman identifies a simultaneous active desire *and* identification experienced by women in the negative Oedipal complex, varying from explicitly choosing the maternal love object in lesbian sexuality to more dispersed processes involving female bonding: 'desire and identification may be strung along a single thread in the female version of the Oedipus complex' (1985: 150). This alternative theoretical position she terms the 'homosexual-maternal fantasmatic' (1985: 125); and is one not subject to cultural disavowal (the process described by Metz where the cinema spectator must simultaneously affirm and deny what is seen on screen), because the already castrated female subject has no need for this psychic mechanism involving separation from the image. Such a critique leads Silverman to identify a split female subject able not only to articulate 'I' but also to speak of an alternative 'libidinal politics'. The 'homosexual-maternal fantasmatic' reveals an alternative position for the female spectator to occupy: namely, a split subject simultaneously defined by recognition (identification), but also a refusal to be enclosed by one unified position. This split subject is always drawn to alternative scenarios of desire, and is used by feminist filmmakers to represent a different kind of desire. Her revision of a founding feminine fantasy contributes enormously to a more troubled and nuanced feminist film theory, as it looks beyond film theories that position women, either as spectators or representation, defined as either 'castrated male' or 'fetishised phallic female'.

Jackie Stacey, focusing on two Hollywood films, *All About Eve* (Joseph Mankiewicz, 1950) and *Desperately Seeking Susan* (Susan Siedelman, 1984), analyses 'a woman's obsession with another woman' (2000: 460). Constructing female identities is a central theme, and active desire generated through one woman becoming more like an idealised feminine other: 'However, the pleasures of this feminine desire cannot be collapsed into simple identification, since difference and otherness are continuously played upon' (2000: 464). This interplay between 'difference and otherness' leads Stacey to conclude that rigid divisions identified by orthodox psychoanalytic models leave little room for understanding female desire and narcissism in relation to another female. While she is criticised by the likes of Teresa de Lauretis for de-eroticising female identification, Stacey defends her critique of homoeroticism as about encompassing 'forms of fascination between women available to *all* women in the cinema' (1994: 29) that generate desire *and* identification on both conscious and unconscious levels (see chapter two).

Conceiving of lesbian subjectivity and desire: Teresa de Lauretis and perverse desire

Practice of Love: Lesbian Sexuality and Perverse Desire by Teresa de Lauretis can be viewed as the culmination of twenty years of feminist interest in psychoanalytic theory with the more recent intervention from queer politics. De Lauretis' latest contribution shifts feminist debate about a desiring female subjectivity away from accounts rooted in a 'homosexual relation to the mother' with its 'fluid or oscillating patterns of identifications and object-choices' (1994: xvii). Rereading Freudian psychoanalysis 'through Laplanche and the Lacanian and feminist revisions (1994: xiii) for theories of representation, subjectivity and desire, and combining it with her thinking on semiotics and the relationship between sexual difference and techniques of cinematic narration discussed in her earlier work (de Lauretis 1984; see chapter one), de Lauretis formulates a theoretical model of perverse desire which opens out 'the psychic and social modalities of lesbian sexuality' (ibid.).

Central to her thinking is what she calls 'Freud's negative theory of sexuality – sexuality as perversion' (1994: xi). Reviewing his work from *Three Essays on the Theory of Sexuality* (1905) to papers he was writing at the time of his death in 1939 prompts her to note that 'notions of a normal sexuality, a normal psychosexual development, even a normal sexual act derive from the detailed consideration of the aberrant, deviant or perverse manifestations and components of the sexual instinct or drive' (1994: xii). Normal sexuality is *only* a projection, belonging to the Symbolic and referring to the successful completion of the Oedipal complex, while 'perversion and neurosis (the repressed form of perversion) are the actual forms and contents of sexuality' (ibid.).

Fantasy plays a crucial structuring role in constituting the sexual subject and desire. Grounding her thinking in Laplanche and Pontalis' idea of fantasy as the staging of desire enables de Lauretis to describe origins of sexuality as structured by fantasy. Primal fantasies (parental coitus, castration) function less as essential truths than as cultural myths, because 'like myths, they claim to provide a representation of, and a solution to, the major enigmas which confront the child' (Laplanche and Pontalis, quoted in de Lauretis 1994: 82). Such thinking helps her reconsider the meaning of castration, to suggest that castration is not about an actual loss but the narcissistic fantasy of loss in relation to body-image.

> I can conclude that the castration complex rewrites in the symbolic as lack of a penis what is a primary narcissistic loss of body-image, a lack of being that threatens the imaginary matrix of the body-ego. On the disavowal of *this* lack depends perverse desire and the formation of a fetishlike object or sign that both lures and signifies the subject's desire, at once displacing and re-signifying the wished-for female body (1994: xviii).

Reformulating castration theory (the fantasy of losing one's own imagined body-image) enables de Lauretis to propose a model of perverse desire.

Lesbian subjectivity is constituted through the fantasy of castration, predicated upon a 'narcissistic wound to the subject's body image' (1994: 264). For the lesbian subject, castration involves a narcissistically loved female body – or her own imagined body-image – which must in turn be disavowed and displaced onto the fetish. Whether the fetish is a butch lesbian or a *femme* exhibiting excessive femininity, it serves not as an actual substitute but represents a signifier of desire within the fantasy scenario:

> Lesbian desire is not the identification with another woman's desire, but the desire for her desire as signified in her fetish and the fantasy scenario it evokes. What one desires is her lover's perverse desire; her fetish, in which her castration or lack of being is both acknowledged and denied, also mediates the other's fantasmatic access to her originally lost body. (1994: 251)

Establishing the psychic processes involved in constituting lesbian subjectivity, de Lauretis further suggests how this 'sexual structuring is both an effect and a condition of the social construction of sexuality' (1994: 309). What is being advanced here is that the subject is constituted through the persistent struggle between the instinctual drives of the id and the superego, and between individual fantasy and the external social world. For de Lauretis, sexual identity is 'dynamically (re)structured by forms of fantasy – private and public, conscious and unconscious – which are culturally available and historically specific' (1994: xix). Her position combines Freudian psychoanalytical theories on the psyche with Foucault's descriptions of how institutional practices implant sexuality into the social body. Noting such an intimate relationship between the sexual and social subject allows her to set out the conditions that make possible lesbian representation (de Lauretis 2000).

Looking at feminist 'guerrilla cinema' and filmmaking practice, de Lauretis identifies new representational strategies producing new knowledges about the lesbian subject and lesbian fantasy scenarios (de Lauretis 1990). Her textual reading of Sheila McLaughlin's *She Must Be Seeing Things* (1987), about 'a lesbian fantasy of origins', explores the difficulties of representing lesbian desire through codes and conventions of dominant cinema imbibed with a heterosexual lexicon (de Lauretis 1994: 85–116). The analysis further explores the difficulties involved in portraying 'a scenario of lesbian *spectatorial* desire and enables the visualization ... of a *lesbian* subject of viewing' (1994: 99–100). Cinema spectatorship emerges as the 'site of articulation of individual subjectivity with social subjecthood, of fantasy with representation, or of private with public fantasies' (1994: 125).

Lesbian authorship and spectatorship: Judith Mayne

Turning to Luce Irigaray's discussion of the troublesome question of female homosexuality read through Freud's case history of Dora, in 'The Psychogenesis of a Case of Homosexuality in a Woman'[7] gives Judith Mayne insight into issues related to 'narration and identification, masculinity and femininity and dominant and alternative practice' that seem 'particularly relevant to lesbian authorship in the cinema' (1990: 119). What Mayne finds intriguing about the famous case study is the problem Dora faced in articulating 'her desire not simply for the loved object, but for a certain staging of that desire' (1990: 121). Mayne identifies similar tensions at work in the films of lesbian/feminist filmmakers. Just as Dora could not escape the heterosexual language of psychoanalysis to make her actions 'readable' (in fact 'the woman's desire for self-annihilation occurs ... [only] when her desire becomes fully representable within conventional terms' (1990: 122)), nor can the lesbian filmmaker avoid cinema's institutionalisation of heterosexual desire. Mayne characterises this in-between space 'both/and' which defines the lesbian position as being both complicit with and resistant to patriarchal fictions. The lesbian filmmaker simultaneously acknowledges and refuses phallocentric norms. 'Lesbian representation highlights contradiction in particularly strong ways, for lesbianism is both lure and threat for patriarchal culture as well as for feminism, and it challenges a model of signification in which masculinity and activity, femininity and passivity, are always symmetrically balanced' (1990: 125).

If lesbian fantasy scenarios are produced in a cinematic apparatus that reproduces patriarchal structures, then neither can the lesbian experience be truly represented on screen. Reconsidering the female authorship of lesbian filmmakers like Dorothy Arzner leads Mayne to claim that the lesbian *auteur* negotiates such a predicament in her films. She identifies in particular a 'lesbian irony' (1990: 115), referring to an iconic juxtaposition of lesbian desire with the cinematic apparatus as 'both complicit with and radically other than the laws of narrative and visual pleasure' (1990: 154). With the lesbian author well versed in how patriarchal culture produces gendered identitites, she is able to both comply and refute 'heterosexual norms' on screen. The most intriguing manifestation of this preoccupation occurs, argues Mayne, in *Christopher Strong* (1933) when Christopher (Colin Clive) declares his love for Cynthia Darrington (Katharine Hepburn. Darrington dresses for a fancy-dress ball as a moth, wearing a 'shimmery, tight dress and headdress complete with antennae', looking ridiculous as a 'cybernetic ant' (1990: 120). Her oscillating femme/romance to butch/career change of clothes quite literally reveals to Mayne how Darrington occupies two distinct worlds. Irony offers not only a challenge to patriarchal institutions in general but also perspectives on female experience and 'female bonding' in particular.

Mayne shares similar conclusion with de Lauretis regarding lesbian spectatorship. She notes how the lesbian spectator locates the cinematic screen as a site of conflict, in which it functions simultaneously to prohibit as well as offer alternative scenarios of desire. Mediating private psychic fantasies with public social ones, and involving an interaction with context and inter-textuality (as Andrea Weiss noted, rumour and gossip constituted the hidden history of the gay subculture; see chapter two), the cinema as a public space played a crucial role in 'the shaping of marginal communities' (1993: 162) and defining identities for them. What interests her in particular is how studying lesbian spectatorship reveals heterosexual presumptions imbibed in the cinematic apparatus alongside 'a critical spectatorship' (how the spectator challenges the dominant reading and makes use of the text in contradictory ways).

Queering the body

Elizabeth Grosz is concerned within rethinking lesbianism and lesbian desire in radically different ways from those previously discussed in this chapter. She feels current scholarship has got it wrong by suggesting that lesbian desire is all about fantasy. She asks if it is possible to identify desire as something other than predicated on absence and acquisition. For her, sexuality and desire are 'energies, excitations, impulses, actions, movements, practices, moments, pulses of feeling' (1994: 182). It is not a question of acquiring identity but about 'the infinite possibilities of becoming' (1994: 226). Borrowing heavily from the Deleuzian concept of 'becoming', Grosz understands desire as about becoming bound with other bodily flows, sexual practices and pleasure for its own sake. Sexuality is 'a truly nomad desire unfettered by anything external, for anything can form part of its circuit, can be absorbed into its operations' (1994: 183). Opening out understanding in this way suggests to Grosz that homosexuality cannot be reduced to a category but points toward possibilities – of unsettling stable categories of sexual difference, of making known the 'fundamental fluidity and transformability of sexuality and its enactment in sexed bodies' (1994: 227).

Grounded in the work of Michel Foucault, feminist scholars working in psychoanalysis and postmodernism studied the body as an object of gendered knowledge (Butler 1990; Grosz 1994). Theorists identified social discourse as responsible for regulating and normalising the gendered body into appropriate and inappropriate sexual behaviour and identities. Judith Butler (1993) in particular notes that all gender identity is regulated through the policing and shaming of sexualities. Disputing Kristéva's relegation of lesbianism to the maternal space of the semiotic enables her to claim that no gendered body exists neither before, nor in opposition to, the Symbolic but belongs to the social world. Heterosexual norms constitute the proper gendered body, predicated on producing homosexuality and gender inversion as abject.

Key to Butler's contribution is what she terms 'gender performativity'. For her, the body does not simply embody social norms but is produced by discourses that give it meaning (Butler 1990; 1993). The concept of performance is central to her thinking, for gender identity is a kind of performance: it is the imitation and impersonation of sexuality. Gender is learnt through repeated performances and involves manipulating codes such as clothes, gestures and behaviour. Yet what is being performed is a 'phantasmatic [an object distorted by perception] ideal of heterosexual identity' (Butler 1991: 21). What this means is that there is no 'natural' or 'original' heterosexual masculinity and femininity (despite what heterosexuality would have us believe); but instead we construct an ideal of it through our performances. Her analysis of *Paris is Burning* (Jennie Livingston, 1991), a film that depicts Black gay drag balls in Harlem, makes the case for suggesting that gender is nothing more than a cultural performance. The self-conscious parody inherent in the drag performance functions as 'a kind of talking back' (1999: 334) to cultural gender norms. Appropriating and exposing the ideals of white femininity means these

Black male performers draw attention to not only how gender ideals are constituted but also to our own complicity with 'a constant and repeated effort to imitate (1999: 338) gender ideals.

The need to constantly perform gender reveals how the 'heterosexual performativity is beset by ... anxiety' (Butler 1999: 338), in that heterosexuality *only* remains the norm through repetitive performances. Homosexuality operates as a self-conscious parody. It is another masquerade that incites a critical disruption of heterosexual norms because it directs awareness to the non-identity of gender identity and sexuality, and to the different sexualities that can be implanted into the body. Alison Butler sums up significance of Butler's intervention:

> What is effected by the introduction of the notion of performativity is the reconceptualisation of gender as a more open field, socially regulated and normalised but liable to change in ways that the Lacanian model, ruled by the monolith of the Symbolic, does not allow. (2000: 74)

The 1980s saw feminist film theory reach maturity as it became institutionalised as an academic discipline – as an object of serious study. It was a period marked by a refining of the theory and concerns that sprang up in the 1970s. Charted above are the key publications that set the agenda for a new range of theoretical knowledge and research possibilities. Such intellectual activity revealed the desire from those writing feminist film theory to produce new conceptual tools which would allow them to move the discourse away from the apparent theoretical stagnation caused by male-dominated theoretical paradigms (such as the negation of feminine sexuality which characterised Lacanian psychoanalytic theory).

Yet the refinement of psychoanalytic feminism by academic feminists laid the film feminism open to charges of abstraction with its theoretical jargon and difficult language. Such a state of affaires led feminist critics like B. Ruby Rich to announce the demise of film feminism: 'What sprang up in the 1970s and was institutionalised in the 1980s has been stagnating in the 1990s, its vigour bypassed by queer culture, on the one hand, multiculturalism on the other, and cultural studies in general' (1998: 5). As the 1980s drew to a close it alarmed many feminists to discover their theoretical endeavours into the omission of the female subject from cinematic pleasures within mainstream cinema confirmed the very arguments they had set out to critique. Theoretical models had ironically contributed to producing another ahistorical, abstracted female subject. Such critical deadlock was precipitated by the burden of needing to legitimise film feminism within the academy. The more scholars endeavoured to map out, identify, and fix the unique field of film feminist inquiry, the more the discipline became 'paralysed by dead ends of its own development' (ibid.). Charges of essentialism led to a stalemate of what has been called postfeminism.

As the 1980s gave way to the 1990s, queer theory and gay/lesbian studies chided feminist film theory not only for its over reliance on psychoanalysis, but also for its restrictive definitions of sexual difference. Theories opposing any claim to a coherent sexual or gender identity gave fresh impetus to discussions around subjectivity, sexual difference and gendered fantasy. Yet these new statements posed another problem. While it usefully exposed a different system of sexual difference – of narrative, viewing practices and visual pleasure – not governed by heterosexual assumptions, the theoretical density of these ideas seemingly led film feminism into an intellectual cul-de-sac.

CONCLUSION

Feminism has no single vision, although it is a visionary way of seeing. (Humm 1997: 3)

[It] is particularly tempting to write a history of feminist theory – precisely because it is feminist – which stresses or even implies 'progress'. Yet, it is important to acknowledge that, even and perhaps especially within feminism, there is the ever present potential of regression, uneven development, failure and disillusion, not to mention misunderstanding. (Bergstrom & Doane 1989: 15)

What this book has aimed to do is identify how feminist film theory came to write the woman into film narrative and cinema practices. Not only did feminist film theory disrupt orthodox wisdom on gender identity and sexual difference, but it also quickly generated theories about female subjectivity and spectating habits, female desire and viewing pleasures, and feminine identities linked to class, sexuality, race and ethnicity. With any given discourse there are specific (and sometimes unwritten) rules that determine what can and cannot be said. Despite the complexity and diversity of opinions outlined in this book, the feminist theoretical project has been underpinned by another kind of desire – the desire to put into discourse the feminine in cinema. Catherine MacKinnon has written 'that feminist theory is the first theory to emerge from those whose interests it affirms' (quoted in Humm 1997: 6). I thus finish this book by sketching the processes and problems involved in making visible the feminist film studies. I suggest that we may in fact have reached a point when it might be more important to gain knowledge about the features of feminist writings on film and cinema; for in understanding what feminist film theory wants us to know exposes the workings of a discourse as well as the difficulties that still remain in articulating it.

Locating a feminine voice

Second-wave feminism did not simply give voice to feminist discontentment but critically intervened to disclose the mechanisms at work in producing knowledge about women under patriarchy. Annette Kuhn notes how feminism interrupted and made known the relationship between power and knowledge involved in constructing gender identities:

> Politics and knowledge are interdependent. In the ordinary way, the link between them will often go unnoticed or be taken for granted: where feminism is concerned, however, this is impossible, precisely because knowledge has had to be self-consciously produced alongside political activity. (1985b: 1–2)

Maggie Humm agrees with Kuhn's position but further suggests it would be impossible to understand how 'gender profoundly shapes cinema' without 'the tangible vision of feminism' (1997: 5).

Since many women attracted to film studies were part of the first generation reared on a popular, visual culture, they were acutely aware of the influence exerted by the image within contemporary culture. Marjorie Rosen (1973) shared with Kate Millett (1970) her Marxist thinking on how ideology works through images to reflect and misrepresent the real socio-political world. Hollywood, as an institution producing dominant representation, endlessly reproduces patriarchal distortions: misrepresentations conveying both male fantasies and anxieties. It is important therefore to grasp how feminist thinking emerged at a time when the number of women participating in the public sphere had increased as never before but discrimination against women continued to persist. Feminist film theory grew out of a need to address the inherent sexism within language and stereotypical images as well as institutions concerned with perpetuating such thinking.

Lost histories and archiving representation

The early 1970s saw a spate of film festivals devoted to showcasing the work of women filmmakers, both past and present. These festivals aimed to retrieve 'her-story', and represented a need to clear the ground. They also gave feminists the opportunity to rewrite film history to include past contributions made by women previously repressed. Searching the archives enabled feminists to reclaim forgotten female *auteurs* such as Alice Guy (pioneer of French cinema and early filmmaker), Lois Weber (early American director), Leontine Sagan and Dorothy Arzner, but also to (hopefully) uncover 'a coherent feminine aesthetic' (Mulvey 1979: 5). It proved to be a depressing state of affairs that validated the discrimination and marginalisation identified in the early studies (Rosen 1973; Haskell 1987). Yet the reason why particular women filmmakers were reclaimed in the first place was dependent on the political agenda. Arzner in particular had immediate appeal. With her alternate (lesbian) lifestyle while working as an editor, writer and director inside the Hollywood dream factory, she was viewed as an excellent example of someone subverting from within. Others such as avant-garde filmmakers like Germaine Dulac and Maya Deren fascinated feminists for the way in which they explored interior (feminine) states and destabilised dominant (male) film forms. Yet other directors like Leni Riefenstahl – a woman who had created representation for an oppressive patriarchal system – appeared to offer nothing. The point here is that what is chosen from the archive to be retrieved and analysed is dependent on how well the filmmaker fits the feminist political world-view.

Another reason for feminist interest in Dorothy Arzner also proves instructive for the feminist film theory discourse. Informed by second-wave feminism, feminist scholars began to look differently at dominant cinema and filmmaking practice. Early theories were consciously put forward as forms of (political) resistance to contemporary analyses of classical Hollywood cinema. In particular, the deliberate *auteurist* approach adopted by Claire Johnston and Pam Cook was in direct response to what they perceived as the existing 'oppressive theory' (Johnston 1973: 26) conceived by male critics working in *auteur* studies who omitted any discussion of the woman, either as image or narrative agent (Sarris 1968; Truffaut 1976; Rivette 1985). The contribution made by those British feminist critics influenced by poststructuralism to the writing of feminist film theory would transform the questions asked by feminists:

The task for feminist criticism must consist of a process of de-naturalisation: a questioning of the unity of text; of seeing it as a contradictory interplay of different codes; of tracing its 'structuring absences' and its relationship to the universal problem of symbolic castration. (Cook & Johnston 1990: 26)

Understanding how ideological contradictions are negotiated primarily through sexual difference enabled scholars like Johnston to not only consider the function of feminist criticism but also put forward a model of an emerging feminist film practice that would counter dominant modes of film production.

Creating representation for a feminist film theory

The other history that frames the beginning of feminist film theory relates to putting the theory into practice. Experimental and documentary film forms proved important in the feminist struggle to find alternative representation, new forums and theories. In West Germany for example, documentaries directed by women in the late-1960s and early-1970s were not only made to address women's absence from cultural production, but also provided an intellectual space where issues such as abortion legislation and the demand for equal pay were voiced. Screenings would often be followed by public debate. Revealed here is how film feminism grew out of political activism, in which a broad alliance of feminist women fought to create new forms, locate sites for the community and write new theories.

New feminist documentaries inspired by independent filmmaking techniques and modes of production, as well as second-wave feminism, rejected stereotypical images of women. Films like Julia Reichert and James Klein's *Growing Up Female* (1971) and Geri Ashur's *Janie's Janie* (1971) dealt with feminist concerns in an immediate and accessible manner (Rosenberg 1983). Direct formal address not only became a means of raising awareness but also gave representation to feminist activism. While not restricted to making documentaries, women's independent filmmaking, with its explicit agenda for dealing with issues that impacted upon women's lives, offered itself up to be analysed by feminist film theory and criticism. Other independent filmmaking initiatives went even further, to explicitly embed theoretical paradigms into the very form and structure of the filmmaking practice. Laura Mulvey's *Riddle of the Sphinx*

(1977, co-directed with Peter Wollen) operates as an aesthetic companion piece to the 'Visual Pleasure and Narrative Cinema' (1975) article. It gives aesthetic form to the critical issues raised in her theoretical work. Arguing that visual pleasure in dominant (Hollywood) cinema draws on narcissism and fetishistic scopophilia, Mulvey devises alternative forms of cinematic representation that seek to interrogate cultural myths of woman and deconstruct unconscious textual relations. Women's cinema continues to contest dominant forms of representation exposed in the writing of a feminist film theory, while feminist film theory makes sense of the alternative filmmaking practice and representational forms produced by women in the process of theorising female subjectivity and spectatorship anew.

Difficulties in speaking

Despite self-confirming parameters that intimately bind feminist film theory to women's cinema in celebration and validation, feminist film studies is vulnerable to self-criticism and theoretical stagnation. Feminist theory, for example, faces a dilemma over its reliance on particular methodologies to describe the woman as Other. Psychoanalysis and semiotics provide invaluable terms and conceptual models that help feminist scholars understand the patriarchal unconscious: 'Psychoanalysis dissolves the veneer of surface meanings; semiotics focus on the split nature of the sign or language itself as the point for change; confrontation with ideology brings up the issue of identification of how a text places a spectator in relation to it' (Mulvey 1979: 9). Yet using psychoanalytic models devised by male authors such as Freud and Lacan, and characterised by the masculine experience of separation and the denial of female subjectivity, comes at a price. Struggling with the language of patriarchy is a precarious task. It is a dilemma anticipated by Laura Mulvey: 'how to fight the unconscious structured like a language (formed critically at the moment of arrival of language) while still caught within the language of the patriarchy' (1975: 7). Feminist academics have thus long been vigilant about the difficulties involved in using methodologies rooted in patriarchal language and male privilege. Self-reflexivity, whereby the scholar interrogates the mechanisms of a theoretical model in the process of applying it, has emerged as a crucial feature of feminist film writing. Maybe it is now worth interrogating the history of the feminist film theory engagement with psychoanalysis for its own sake, not only to consider the compulsive desire to return to theoretical models that degrade and/or exclude woman, but to understand more fully the development of these feminist texts that seek to breakdown the tyranny of dominant discourses.

B. Ruby Rich, in her latest book, *Chick Flicks: Theories and Memories of the Feminist Film Movement*, views feminist film culture as reaching something of a critical impasse in recent years. While her central thesis stresses the need for the current generation to reconnect with the activism of 1970s film theory and the sense of 'lived experience now forgotten, shelved, or denied by those who went through them' (1998: 1), her observation indicates how feminist film theory engages in its own acts of repression, both conscious and unconscious, in the process of asserting its right to speak. As one particular theoretical position develops and refines thinking, another comes along to discredit and render its findings questionable, if not irrelevant. Feminists from the second generation chide those from the first for their ahistorical essentialism while revisionist cultural studies scholars accuse their predecessors of relativism and a 'political and theoretical naiveté' (Modleski 1998: 2). Janet Bergstrom (1990) goes as far to note the virtual deletion of 1970s film theory from feminist publications by the end of the 1980s. Each new generation appears to reproach the other in the process of seeking out sameness and a common ground shared by women. Processes concerned with discrediting, and separating out from, past feminist debates reveal the perils involved in policing the feminist project. Understanding the question of credibility and whose critical approach gets legitimated and how is an important undertaking for feminist film theory in the future.

Christine Gledhill writes that 'criticism represents the profession-alisation of meaning production' (1988: 74). Recognising the role of the feminist film scholar/critic to confer meaning, as a theme underlying feminist film theory, is another issue worth exploring. Feminist scholars like Ien Ang theorise the ambivalence of their role as interpreter: 'this ambivalence is on the one hand connected with my identity as an intellectual and a feminist, and on the other hand with the fact that I have always particularly like watching soap operas like *Dallas*' (1996: 12). Tania Modleski, on the other hand, is concerned with 'transformations occurring in women's genres and looks at the way new realities, or new critiques of existing realities, are being articulated in forms familiar and pleasurable to masses of women (1998: 10). She is someone not only seeking to 'change women stories' in her own work as an author but interested in locating new approaches to help the feminist critic interpret the changes that are occurring in women's cultural production. For others like Lola Young it is imperative for those underrepresented in the academy and traditionally marginalised such as Black women to assert their right to speak and take the lead in defining the debate.

> Although nothing is guaranteed by the presence of Black women filmmakers or critics, it is important for them to be empowered to make more interventions in the construction and criticism of images in Britain … is especially important for black people to become involved in the analysis of media and culture and to produce knowledge and cultural theory in order to challenge the hegemony of white and male critics. (1996: 181)

Demonstrating a self-conscious awareness of the feminist critic's role in constructing meaning reveals another site where intellectual contestation is made known. Talking about writing a theory allows scholars to recognise limits – the insufficiencies of existing methodologies to offer adequate explanations of woman – and use their own voice to disrupt and question from the outside or on the margins. Often these voices evoke an exile from the language with which feminists are using to write the theory. Exile here does not mean separation but rather a condition where the scholar can develop skills to think in daring new ways.

Studying feminist film theory as discourse

I identify feminist film theory as a discourse; that is, a discursive formation made up from a series of statements within which, and by which, debates related to gendered representation, female subjectivity and spectatorship can be known. Foucault's notion of discourse as a circumscribed field of knowledge and power is central to this project. According to him, nothing 'exists' simply to be talked about. Rather, it is through discourse by which something becomes known. By analysing the statements that constitute the making of a field of knowledge, we can see how the speakers and listeners, writers and readers come to know who they are within the social world. Studying discourse requires an understanding of the social and cultural areas through which a field of knowledge is determined. We have reached a point where histories and readers about feminist film studies are now being published (including this contribution). Such works assess and make known the contribution made by feminist film theory to modern thought. I share with Bergstrom (1990) a concern with reclaiming the theoretical context for feminist film theory, and what I have attempted to do here is offer a history of the intellectual formation of the discourse known as feminist film theory. Each chapter identifies a dominant strain – poststructuralism, psychoanalysis, cultural studies, post-colonial theory and postmodernism – shaping a particular theoretical argument and how and why it was said. Returning each theoretical position to its intellectual and historical founding moment is designed to give students a better sense of what is being argued when the vocabulary used by each may now appear obsolete and the terms of reference obscure.

Recent postmodern feminist interventions suggest the arguments have now been won and that there is no longer any need for activism or theory. Such logic is caused in part by the disintegration of a radical political platform; in part because of internal difficulties, whereby an 'elimination of historical understanding' has precipitated charges that 'film theory has somehow failed or come to an end' (Petro 2002: 173); in part because dominant ideology has absorbed dissident feminine voices; and in part because the discourse has moved from the margins and political activism to academic respectability (as Mary Ann Doane queries, 'how has feminist film criticism, which was marginal and controversial at the outset, come to be seen so quickly as an orthodoxy, a monolithic enterprise?' (in Bergstrom and Doane 1989: 15)). If feminist film theory could be read as an Oedipal narrative, then could it not be argued that postmodern feminism is a moment of castration predicated on denial and repression? But the questions raised (and repressed) over the four decades still prove difficult with potentially un-containable elements threatening to erupt into neurotic symptoms within the feminist discourse itself.

Finally I suggest that the feminist film theory is prone to hysteria. What I mean by this is that the feminist film theory can often appear hysterical as a result of being constructed from methodologies that negate female subjectivity and consign women's stories to the category of fantasy (despite Freud's claims to the contrary, suppose the women's tales in 'A Child Is Being Beaten' are really about abuse and incest?). Given the current resistance toward theory and the suspect accorded to the term 'feminism' it is not too surprising that women still face difficulties when attempting to speak under the sway of patriarchy. The more feminist film theory gains respectability within the academy, the more its methodological differences/difficulties are revealed as problems of legitimacy and credibility in speaking from inside the discipline. It is discourse about (rather than in) crisis, in which the female subject – as film protagonist, cinema spectator and academic scholar – continues to trouble. Maybe Michèle Montrelay (1978) is right to claim that the only way to handle this theme of crisis is to continue to be analysed; that is, to locate a critical space whereby the discourse of feminist film studies can repeatedly be discussed.

NOTES

Chapter one

1   Reading Marxist theories through Lacan, Marxist philosopher Louis Althusser
    defines ideology as a system of representations – 'images, myths, ideas or con-
    cepts'. For him, ideology is not about what people consciously believe. Instead, it is
    a process in which individuals are constituted as subject through an unconscious
    network of representational systems called ISA (Institutional State Apparatus).
    Subjects are given images to identify with, and these are communicated through
    ISAs (including church, family, schools, the media). Integral to this process is how
    the ISA 'interpellates' (to confer identity) the individual into accepting their social
    roles and identities as natural and obvious (see Althusser 1971).

2   Category five of Comolli and Narboni's typology: 'films which seem at first sight
    to belong firmly within the ideology and to be completely under its sway, but
    which turn out to be so only in an ambiguous manner ... The films we are talking
    about throw up obstacles in the way of the ideology, causing it to swerve and
    get off course. The cinematic framework lets us see it, but also shows it up and
    denounces it ... An internal criticism is taking place which cracks the film apart
    at the seams. If one reads the film obliquely, looking for symptoms; if one looks
    beyond its apparent formal coherence, one can see that it is riddled with cracks: it
    is splitting under the internal tension which is simply not there in an ideologically
    innocuous film' (Comolli & Narboni 1971: 33). What Comolli and Narboni suggest is
    that some films offer themselves particularly well to ideological analysis because
    they are already marked by disruption in relation to ideology. This disturbance is
    identifiable through textual 'symptoms' – breaks or contradictions within the text.
    Identifying those elements which the text has chosen to exclude or repress for the

3 An early example of ideological analysis from the *Cahiers du cinéma* editors was the reading of *Young Mr Lincoln* (1976). Analysing the concealed ideological work in this classical Hollywood text, they identify a text ruptured through a series of structuring absences. Omitting any signs of his involvement with the abolition of slavery that complicates his position in history means the film could elevate Lincoln to mythical status. However, the issue of slavery is not lost but instead returns in a displaced form, repeated – in the soundtrack that incorporates the patriotic song of the South – as a musical motif.

sake of ideological coherence allows the critic not only to gain insight into how ideology constructs meaning but also what it wants to hide.

4 Roland Barthes applied semiotics as a critical tool to expose how ideology transmits its meaning through cultural texts and practices while concealing the mechanisms of its own operation. Ideology, or what he calls 'myth', functions to drain the sign (the text or practice) of its primary (denotative) meaning, to replace it with a symbolic (connotative) one. Jacqueline Rose describes Barthes' semiotic theory as marking a shift from 'the analysis of the structure of language' (1988: 142) to a critique of the unstable nature of the sign – the actual word/image.

5 Alison Butler extends the implications of Johnston's thinking for feminist aesthetics and an emergence Women's Cinema; see Butler (2003) *Women's Cinema: The Contested Screen*. London: Wallflower Press.

6 The Imaginary: 'mirror phase'. Early developmental stage when the child (aged between six and eighteen months) begins to recognise itself as an individual based on a moment of looking. Primary identification (the formation of ego) finds the child jubilantly caught up in an image beyond itself. On first seeing itself in a mirror or other images, and able to sense separation from other bodies (its mother or father), the infant identifies with and assimilates the mirror-image that seems gratifyingly whole and in control unlike its own uncoordinated body: from 'fragmented body-image to a form to its totality' (Lacan 1977: 4). Thus the child internalises the other's otherness as Ideal. Identification with the mirror-image – involving not only separation from others but also a misrecognition of the self as unified – defines the child's experience prior to the entry into language. Furthermore, this moment when the child experiences (or misinterprets) narcissistic attachment to the mirror image is also a moment of self-alienation, of rupture, for the infant is identifying with an image that is forever somewhere else as well as that of another. The process of subject formation is structured by a series of irreconcilables, distortions and misunderstandings involving the gazing subject and the pleasurable spectacle (objectification) of the self as coherent.

7 The Symbolic: Lacan understood the Symbolic as the social, cultural and linguistic

networks into which the child is born. These laws, rules, codes and prohibitions exist prior to the child, and are those to which they must submit in order to enter society.

8   Freud's essay on (male) sexuality: The (male) child gains knowledge of sexual difference predicated on the shocking sight of absence: the lack of a penis on the female body precipitates a belief in the male child that castration can occur. Disavowal: To counter the perceived castration threat the child disavows sexual difference and the (m)Other's lack, reasoned as the absent maternal phallus. Never quite being able to suppress the belief that the woman does in fact possess a penis, despite knowing of its absence, gives rise to fetishism. Fetishism: Acts as a form of psychic protection against castration anxiety. The male child gains pleasure from a substitute object (a fetish) that simultaneously hides the lack – an illusion of the object as complete – while its very presence at the same time is a constant reminder of lack.

9   Revising the Freudian orthodoxy, Lacan explains how we come to know who we are is structured by and through the acquisition of language. The world of language precedes us; it is associated with others (a place where an external speaker hears and responds to us), and demands that we take up pre-assigned identities and social roles; it constitutes us at the same time as we assert ourselves as speaking subjects within it. In and through such a process, the child's knowledge of sexual difference is predicated on a privileging of the patriarch within the symbolic order. The father is not a real person but a metaphor within the Symbolic: name of the father, or the Law of the Father serves as a symbolic function that allows the male infant both to enter into the symbolic order and to master language while repressing the feminine.

Chapter two

1   Anthropologist Claude Lévi-Strauss worked to understand rules governing kinship relationships as well as the function of myth within traditional (or 'primitive') societies. Stripping away the surface layer of myth led him to expose the contradictions at work in any given social structure.

2   Antonio Gramsci's theory of 'hegemony' refers to the ever-shifting play of ideological, social and political forces through which power is opposed and sustained. It is the processes involved in how the dominant (bourgeois) social group maintains authority over a subordinate one through mobilising consent rather than force. Cohesion and persuasion are used to disseminate a social reality that is considered 'common sense'. The field of culture emerges as crucial to this process. It is

a site of constant struggle, especially since Gramsci recognises that hegemony is never secure but in a constant state of flux and open to negotiation between contesting groups.

Chapter three

1   Said defines 'Orientialism as a discourse' (1978: 3), suggesting that the West came to define its boundaries and assert cultural dominance from the eighteenth century onwards through institutionalising knowledge of Europe's 'Other' – the Orient. He refers to a *latent* Orientalism (fantasies, myths, obsessions) and *manifest* Orientalism (philosophy, anthropology) that constitute how the West came to know the Orient, culminating in Imperialism and the idea of Empire. In the process of knowing the Orient, the West asserted its imperial authority (explained European supremacy and the importance of Western civilisation) and justified its right to rule through strategies of intervention and institutions (law, colonial administration, civil service, army).

2   For Foucault, discourse is not a text but a set of statements within which, and by which, the world comes to be known. Knowledge and 'truth', constituted in language and representation, is determined by institutions that hold power and is tied to particular historical moments.

Chapter four

1   New French Feminisms were influenced by Lacan's recognition that sexuality is constituted in discourse, constructed from language, and combined with the semiotic tradition most strongly associated with Barthes. These continental philosophers saw theory 'as a masculine fantasy to which the only response ... is the dissolution, not just of institutions, but of language itself' (Rose 1988: 3).

2   Early libidinal development is the same for both sexes: firstly, both experience pleasurable sensations from erotogenic zones (the penis and clitoris respectively); and both take the mother as the first love object. However as the child approaches the Oedipal stage, the girl needs to accept her own 'castration', and transfer her desire from the mother (also castrated) to the father (associated with penis envy) and later his substitutes with whom she can have a child. At this stage, the girl child must abandon the (phallic) clitoris, and accept feminine passivity as normal.

3   Michèle Montrelay describes that while it is possible for the male to displace his first love object, the female has no choice but to be the object of desire: 'Recovering herself as maternal body (and also as phallus), the woman can no

long repress, "lose", the first stake of representation … From now on, anxiety, tied to the presence of this body, can only be insistent, continuous. This body, so close, which she has to occupy, is an object in excess which must be "lost", that is to say, repressed, in order to be symbolised' (1978: 91–2).

4   Riviere's analysis of a heterosexual intellectual female patient results in her theory of female masquerade. It describes the masquerade of femininity as an excessive, compulsive impersonation of feminine demeanour and accoutrements, in which the heterosexual woman hides her masculinity complex and penis envy in relation to men: 'Womanliness … could be assumed and worn as a mask, both to hide the possession of masculinity and to avert the reprisals expected if she was found to possess it' (1986: 38). But Riviere goes further to suggest that masquerade is a strategy inherent to the feminine psyche, to mask her active original wishes: 'The reader may now ask how I define womanliness or where I draw the line between genuine womanliness and the masquerade. My suggestion is that … they are the same thing' (ibid.).

5   'Fantasy and the Origins of Sexuality' explores the role played by fantasy in constituting human sexuality. Firstly, drives *only* become properly sexual through their representation in fantasy. This occurs when the subject disengages from an external object (mother's breast) and 'moves into the field of fantasy and by that very fact becomes sexuality' (Laplanche & Pontalis 1986: 25). Fantasy is inextricably linked with desiring an absent object. Yet fantasy is not about retrieving 'the object of desire, but its setting. In fantasy the subject does not pursue the object or its sign: he appears caught up himself in the sequence of images. He forms no representation of the desired object but is himself represented as participating in the scene' (1986: 26). What needs to be grasped here is that fantasy is about staging desire. It is about creating a *mise-en-scène* in which the individual 'is himself represented as participating in the scene' without having 'any fixed place' (ibid.) within the fantasy. Secondly, fantasy scenarios have multiple points of entry ('A Child is Being Beaten' is a good example of seduction fantasy with 'multiple entries' (1986: 23) in which the individual assumes several positions at once). Subject positions are not stable but shift across boundaries of gender identity, sexual preference and biological sex. Another feature identified by Laplanche and Pontalis is how fantasy involves 'a profound continuity between the various fantasy scenarios – the stage-setting of desire – ranging from the daydream to the fantasies recovered or reconstructed by analytic investigation' (1986: 28). Furthermore, fantasies are structured by three 'original' fantasies (*fantasmes originaires*) or fantasies of origins: 1) primal scene (imagining parental coitus relates to one's beginnings); 2) fantasies of seduction (relates to origins of sexuality); 3) fantasies of castration

(relates to origins of sexual difference). In addition, secondary fantasies (like day-dreams) endlessly revise original fantasies with 'kaleidoscopic material' (1986: 13) taken from everyday experience. In sum, the origin of the sexual subject is rooted 'in the field of fantasy' (1986: 19) where the need for the lost object becomes representation.

6   Looking to psychoanalysis and semiotic theories (especially Barthes), Kristéva focuses on the acquisition of language and object relation theory involving the interaction between mother and child. She identifies the semiotic (or chora) – a pre-symbolic realm of the (female) body, of gesture, of rhythm, of sensual experience – as simultaneously the realm of the feminine (the maternal) and the realms that exerts pressure on the Symbolic. This idea – a pre-symbolic realm that exists prior to language and poses a disruptive threat to the Symbolic – has proved attractive for feminists as well as being subject to charges of essentialism.

7   'The Psychogenesis of a Case of Homosexuality in a Woman' (1920). Dora was brought to Freud by her parents because of her love for a (lesbian) prostitute ten years her senior and attempted suicide. Freud's interpretation over Dora's story finds details unanalysed and Freud describing Dora's same-sex infatuation as about expressed hostility toward her father. Freud defines female homosexuality as about a masculine attitude toward the love object (otherwise known as a 'baby butch') (Freud 1977c).

BIBLIOGRAPHY

Althusser, L. (1971) 'Ideology and Ideological State Apparatuses', in *Lenin and Philosophy*. Trans. B. Brewster. London: New Left Books.

Ang, I. (1989) 'Wanted: Audiences. On the Politics of Empirical Audiences Studies', in E. Seiter, H. Borchers, G. Kreutzner and E-M Warth (eds), *Remote Control: Television, Audiences and Cultural Power*. London and New York: Routledge, 96–115.

____ (1996) *Watching Dallas: Soap Opera and the Melodramatic Imagination*. London and New York: Routledge.

Appardurai, A. (1993) 'The Heart of Whiteness', *Callaloo*, 16, 4, 796–807.

Barthes, R. (1973) *Mythologies*. London: Paladin.

Baudry, J-L. (1986a) 'Ideological Effects of the Basic Cinematographic Apparatus' [1970], in P. Rosen (ed.) *Narrative, Apparatus, Ideology*. New York: Columbia University Press, 286–98.

____ (1986b) 'The Apparatus' [1975], in P. Rosen (ed.) *Narrative, Apparatus, Ideology*. New York: Columbia University, 299–318.

Bean, J. M. and D. Negra (2002) *A Feminist Reader in Early Cinema*. Durham and London: Duke University Press.

Bellour, R. (1972) *The Birds: Analysis of a Sequence*. London: British Film Institute.

____ (1977) 'Hitchcock, The Enunciator', *Camera Obscura*, 2, 72–8.

Bergstrom, J. (1979) 'Rereading the work of Claire Johnston', *Camera Obscura*, 3/4, 21–31.

____ (1990) 'American Feminism and French Film Theory', *Iris*, 10, 183–97.

Bergstrom, J. and Doane, M. A. (1989) 'The Female Spectator: Contexts and Directions', *Camera Obscura*, 20/21, 5–27.

Bhabha, H. (1984) 'Of Mimicry and Man: The Ambivalence of Colonial Discourse', *October*, 28, 125–36.

____ (1992) 'The Other Question: the Stereotype and Colonial Discourse' (1983), in

M. Merck (ed.) *The Sexual Subject: A Screen Reader on Sexuality*. London and New York: Routledge, 312–31.

____ (1994) *The Location of Culture*. London and New York: Routledge.

Bobo, J. (1988) '*The Color Purple*: Black Women as Cultural Readers', in E. D. Pribram (ed.) *Female Spectators: Looking at Film and Television*. London and New York: Verso, 90–109.

____ (1989) *Camera Obscura*, 20/21, 100–3.

____ (1993) 'Reading Through the Text: The Black Woman as Audience', in M. Diawara (ed.) *Black American Cinema*. London and New York: Routledge, 272–86.

____ (1995) *Black Women as Cultural Readers*. New York: Columbia University Press.

Brunsdon, C. (1981) '*Crossroads*: Notes on Soap Opera', *Screen*, 22, 4, 32–7.

____ (1989) 'Text and Audience', in E. Seiter, H. Borchers, G. Kreutzner and E-M. Warth (eds) *Remote Control: Television, Audiences and Cultural Power*. London and New York: Routledge, 116–29.

Brunsdon, C., J. D'Acci and L. Spigel (eds) (1997) *Feminist Television Criticism: A Reader*. Oxford: Clarendon Press.

Butler, A. (2000) 'Feminist Theory and Women's Films at the Turn of the Century', *Screen*, 41, 1, 73–9.

____ (2002) *Women's Cinema: The Contested Screen*. London: Wallflower Press.

Butler, J. (1990) *Gender Trouble: Feminism and the Subversion of Identity*. New York and London: Routledge.

____ (1991) 'Imitation and Gender Insurbordination', in D. Fuss (ed.) *Inside/Out: Lesbian Theories, Gay Theories*. New York and London: Routledge, 13–31.

Butler, J. (1993) *Bodies That Matter: On the Discursive Limits of 'Sex'*. New York and London: Routledge.

____ (1999) 'Gender is Burning: Questions of Appropriation and Subversion' [1993], in S. Thornham (ed.) *Feminist Film Theory: A Reader*. New York: New York University Press, 336–49.

Cahiers du cinéma Editors (1976) 'John Ford's *Young Mr Lincoln*' [1971], in B. Nichols (ed.) *Movies and Methods: An Anthology*. Berkeley: University of California Press, 494–528.

Camera Obscura (1976) 'Feminism and Film: Critical Approaches', 1, 3–10.

Carby, H. (1982) 'White Woman Listen! Black Feminism and the Boundaries of Sisterhood', in *The Empire Strikes Back: Race and Racism in 70s Britain*. London: Hutchinson, 212–35.

Carby, H. (1987) *Reconstructing Womanhood*. Oxford: Oxford University Press.

Chodorow, N. (1978) *The Reproduction of Mothering*. Berkeley: University of California Press.

Christian, B. (1985) *Black Feminist Criticism*. Oxford: Pergamon.

____ (1989) 'But What Do We Think We're Doing Anyway? The State of Black Feminist Criticism(s) or My Version of a Little Bit of History', in C. A. Wall (ed.) *Changing*

Our Own Words: Essays on Criticism, Theory and Writing by Black Women. New Brunswick: Rutgers University Press, 58–74

Cixous, H. (1980) 'The Laugh of the Medusa', in E. Marks and I. De Courtivron (eds) *New French Feminisms*. Amherst: University of Massachusetts Press, 245–64.

Clover, C. (1993) *Men, Women and Chainsaws: Gender in the Modern Horror Film*. London: British Film Institutte.

Cohen, S. and I. R. Hark (eds) (1993) *Screening the Male*. London: Routledge.

Combahee River Collective (1986) *The Combahee River Collective Statement*. New York: Kitchen Table Press/Women of Color.

Comolli, J-L. and J. Narboni (1971) 'Cinema/Ideology/Criticism', *Screen*, 12, 1, 27–35.

Cook, P. (1983) 'Melodrama and the Women's Picture', in S. Aspinall and R. Murphy (eds) *Gainsborough Melodrama*. BFI Dossier Number 18. London: British Film Institute, 14–28.

____ (1988) 'Approaching the work of Dorothy Arzner' [1975], in C. Penley (ed.) *Feminism and Film Theory*. London and New York: Routledge, 46–56.

Cook, P. and C. Johnston (1990) 'The Place of Women in the Cinema of Raoul Walsh', in P. Erens (ed.) *Issues in Feminist Film Criticism*. Bloomington: Indiana University Press, 19–27.

Cowie, E. (1989) *Camera Obscura*, 20/21, 127–32.

____ (1993) 'Women, Representation and the Image', in M. Alvarado, E. Buscombe and R. Collins (eds) *The Screen Education Reader*. London: Macmillan, 48–60.

____ (1997) *Representing the Woman: Cinema and Psychoanalysis*. Basingstoke and London: Macmillan.

Creed, B. (1987) 'From Here to Modernity: Feminism and Postmodernism', *Screen*, 28, 2, 47–67.

____ (1990) *The Monstrous Feminine: Film, Feminism and Psychoanalysis. London: Routledge*.

de Beauvoir, S. (1984) *The Second Sex*. London: Penguin.

de Lauretis, T. (1984) *Alice Doesn't: Feminism, Semiotics, Cinema*. Bloomington: Indiana University Press.

____ (1990) 'Guerrilla in the Midst: Women's Cinema in the 80s', *Screen*, 31, 1, 6–25.

____ (1994) *The Practice of Love: Lesbian Sexuality and Perverse Desire*. Bloomington: Indiana University Press.

____ (2000) 'Sexual Indifference and Lesbian Representation' [1988], in E. A. Kaplan (ed.) *Feminism and Film*. Oxford: Oxford University Press, 384–406.

Deutsch, H. (1932) 'On Female Homosexuality'. Trans. E. B. Jackson, *Psychoanalytic Quarterly*, 1, 484–510.

Doane, M. A. (1987) *The Desire to Desire: The Woman's Film of the 1940s*. Basingstoke and London: Macmillan.

____ (1991) *Femmes Fatales: Feminism, Film Theory, Psychoanalysis*. London and New York: Routledge.

____ (2000a) 'Woman's Stake: Filming the Female Body' [1981], in E. A. Kaplan (ed.) *Feminism and Film*. Oxford: Oxford University Press, 86–99.

____ (2000b) 'Film and the Masquerade: Theorising the Female Spectator' [1982], in E. A. Kaplan (ed.) *Feminism and Film*. Oxford: Oxford University Press, 418–36.

Doane, M. A., P. Mellencamp and L. Williams (1984) 'Feminist Film Criticism: An Introduction', in M. A. Doane, P. Mellencamp and L. Williams (eds) *Re-vision: Essays in Film Criticism*. Los Angeles: American Film Institute, 1–17.

Doty, A. (1990) 'The Cabinet of Lucy Ricardo: Lucille Ball's Star Image', *Cinema Journal*, 29, 4, 3–22.

Dyer, R. (1993) 'White' [1988], in *The Matter of Images. Essays on Representation*. London and New York: Routledge, 141–63.

Fanon, F. (1986) *Black Skin, White Masks* [1952]. London: Pluto Press.

Figes, E. (1970) *Patriarchal Attitudes*. Greenwich: Fawcett Publications.

Firestone, S. (1979) *The Dialectic of Sex: The Case for Feminist Revolution*. London: The Women's Press.

Foucault, M. (1981) *The History of Sexuality, Volume 1: An Introduction*. Trans. R. Hurley. London: Penguin.

____ (1985) *The Use of Pleasure, Volume 2 of the History of Sexuality*. Trans. R. Hurley. London: Penguin.

____ (1986) *The Care of the Self, Volume 3 of the History of Sexuality*. Trans. R. Hurley. London: Penguin.

Franklin, S, C. Lury and J. Stacey (1991) 'Feminism and Cultural Studies: Pasts, Presents, Futures', in S. Franklin, C. Lury and J. Stacey (eds) *Off Centre: Feminism and Culture Studies*. London and New York: HarperCollins, 1–19.

Freud, S. (1977a) 'Fetishism' [1927], in *On Sexuality: Three Essays on the Theory of Sexuality and Other Works*. London: Penguin, 345–58.

____ (1977b) *On Sexuality: Three Essays on the Theory of Sexuality and Other Works*. London: Penguin.

____ (1977c) 'Analysis of a Phobia in a Five-Year Old Boy', in *Case Histories 1: 'Dora' and 'Little Hans'*. London: Penguin, 165–305.

____ (1986) 'Femininity' [1933], in *The Essentials of Psychoanalysis: The Definitive Collection of Sigmund Freud's Writing*. London: Pelican Books, 412–32.

____ (2001) 'A Child Is Being Beaten' [1919], in *The Standard Edition of the Complete Psychological Works of Sigmund Freud. Volume XVII (1917–1919): An Infantile Neurosis and Other Works*. London: Vintage, 179–204.

Friedan, B. (1965) *The Feminine Mystique*. London: Penguin.

Friedberg, A. (1993) *Window Shopping: Cinema and the Postmodern*. Berkeley: University of California Press.

Fuss, D. (1993) 'Freud's Fallen Women: Identification, Desire and 'A Case of Homosexuality in a Woman', *Yale Journal of Criticism*, 6, 1, 1–23.

Gaines, J. (2000) 'White Privilege and Looking Relations: Race and Gender in Feminist

Film Theory (1988)', in E. A. Kaplan (ed.) *Feminism and Film*. Oxford: Oxford University Press, 336–55.

Gallop, J. (1981) 'Phallus/Penis: Same Difference', in J. Todd (ed.) *Men by Women: Women and Literature II*, New York and London: Holmes and Meier, 243–51.

Gilman, S. (1985) 'Black Bodies, White Bodies: Toward an Iconography of Female Sexuality in Late Nineteenth-Century Art, Medicine and Literature', *Critical Inquiry*, 12, 1, 228–35.

Gilroy, P. (1993) *The Black Atlantic: Modernity and Double Consciousness*. Cambridge: Harvard University Press.

Gledhill, C. (1978) 'Recent Developments in Feminist Criticism', *Quarterly Review of Film Studies*, 13, 4, 457–93.

____ (ed.) (1987) *Home is Where the Heart Is: Studies in Melodrama and the Woman's Film*. London: British Film Institute.

____ (1988) 'Pleasurable Negotiations', in E. D. Pribram (ed.) *Female Spectators: Looking at Film and Television*. London and New York: Verso, 64–89.

Gray, A. (1992) *Video Playtime: The Gendering of a Leisure Technology*. London and New York: Routledge.

Greer, G. (1971) *The Female Eunuch*. St Albans: Granada Publishing.

Grosz, E. (1994) *Volatile Bodies*. Bloomington: Indiana University Press.

____ (1995) *Space, Time, and Perversion*. New York and London: Routledge.

Hall, S. (1980) 'Encoding/Decoding', in S. Hall, D. Hobson, A. Lowe and P. Willis (eds) *Culture, Media, Language*. London: Hutchinson, 128–38.

Hansen, M. (1983) 'Early Cinema: Whose Public Space', *New German Critique*, 29, 147–84.

____ (1990) 'Adventures of Goldilocks: Spectatorship, Consumerism and Public Life', *Camera Obscura*, 22, 51–72.

____ (1991) *Babel and Babylon: Spectatorship in American Silent Film*. Cambridge: Harvard University Press.

____ (2000) 'Pleasure, Ambivalence, Identification: Valentino and Female Spectatorship', in E. A. Kaplan (ed.) *Feminism and Film*. Oxford: Oxford University Press. 226–45.

Haskell, M. (1987) *From Reverence to Rape: The Treatment of Women in the Movies*. Chicago: University of Chicago Press.

Herzog, C and J. M. Gaines (1985) '"Puffed Sleeves before Tea-Time": Joan Crawford, Adrian and Women Audiences', *Wide Angle*, 6, 4, 24–33.

Hobson, D. (1982) *Crossroads: The Drama of Soap Opera*. London: Methuen.

hooks, b. (1992) *Black Looks: Race and Representation*. London: Turnaround.

____ (1993) 'The Oppositional Gaze: Black Female Spectators', in M. Diawara (ed.) *Black American Cinema*. London and New York: Routledge, 288–302.

Humm, M. (1997) *Feminism and Film*. Edinburgh: Edinburgh University Press.

Irigaray, L. (1985a) *Speculum of the Other Woman*. Trans. G. C. Gill. New York: Cornell

University Press.

____ (1985b) *This Sex Which Is Not One*. Trans. C. Porter. Ithaca: Cornell University.

Jacobs, L. (1997) *The Wages of Sin: Censorship and the Fallen Woman Film, 1928–1942*. Berkeley: University of California Press.

Jermyn, D. (2004) 'In Love With Sarah Jessica Parker: Celebrating Female Fandom and Friendship in *Sex and the City*', in K. Akass and J. McCabe (eds) *Reading Sex and the City: Critical Approaches*. London: IB Tauris, 201–18.

Johnston, C. (1973) 'Introduction', in C. Johnston (ed.) *Notes on Women's Cinema*. London: Society for Education in Film and Television, 2–4.

____ (ed.) (1975) *The Work of Dorothy Arzner: Towards a Feminist Film Criticism*. London: BFI.

____ (2000a) 'Women's Cinema as Counter-Cinema' [1973], in E. A. Kaplan (ed.) *Feminism and Film*. Oxford: Oxford University Press, 22–33.

____ (2000b) 'Dorothy Arzner: Critical Strategies' [1975], in E. A. Kaplan (ed.) *Feminism and Film*. Oxford: Oxford University Press, 139–48.

Joseph, G. (1981) 'The Incompatible *Menage à Trois*: Marxism, Feminism and Racism', in L. Sargent (ed.) *Women and Revolution*. Boston: South End Press, 9–10.

Kaplan, E. A. (1983) *Women and Film: Both Sides of the Camera*. New York and London: Methuen.

____ (1993) 'The Couch-Affair: Gender, Race and the Hollywood Transference', *American Imago*, Winter, 481–514.

____ (1997) *Looking for the Other: Feminism, Film and the Imperial Gaze*. London and New York: Routledge.

____ (ed.) (2000) *Feminism and Film*. Oxford: Oxford University Press.

____ (2000) 'Is the Gaze Male?' in E. A. Kaplan (ed.) *Feminism and Film*. Oxford: Oxford University Press, 119–38.

Kofman, S. (1980) 'Ex: The Woman's Enigma', *Enclitic*, 4, 2, 17–28.

Kristéva, J. (1982) *Powers of Horror: An Essay on Abjection*. New York: Columbia University Press.

____ (1986) 'About Chinese Women', in T. Moi (ed.) *The Kristeva Reader*. Oxford: Blackwell, 138–59.

____ (1987) *Tales of Love*. Trans. L. Roudiez. New York: Columbia University Press.

Kuhn, A. (1985a) *Women's Pictures: Feminism and Cinema*. London: Routledge and Kegan Paul.

____ (1985b) *The Power of the Image: Essays on Representation and Sexuality*. London: Routledge and Kegan Paul.

____ (1992) 'Women's Genres [1983]', in M. Merck (ed.) *The Sexual Subject: A Screen Reader on Sexuality*. London and New York: Routledge, 301–11.

____ (2002) *An Everyday Magic: Cinema and Cultural Memory*. London: I. B. Tauris.

Lacan, J. (1977) *Écrits: A Selection*. Trans. A. Sheridan. London: Tavistock Publications.

____ (1982) *Female Sexuality*. Trans. J. Rose, J. Mitchell and J. Rose (eds). New York and

London: W. W. Norton.

Laplanche, J. and J-B. Pontalis (1986) 'Fantasy and the Origins of Sexuality' [1964], in V. Burgin, J. Donald and C. Kaplan (eds) *Formations of Fantasy*. London and New York: Routledge, 5–34.

Lebeau, V. (1995) *Lost Angels: Psychoanalysis and Cinema*. London and New York: Routledge.

_____ (2001) *Psychoanalysis and Cinema: The Play of Shadows*. London: Wallflower Press.

Lorde, A. (1982) *Zami*. London: Sheba Press.

_____ (1984) *Sister Outsider*. Trumansburg, NY: Crossing Press.

_____ (1988) *A Burst of Light*. London: Sheba Press.

Lyotard, J-F. (1993) *Le Différend*. Paris: Les Editions de Minuit.

MacCabe, C. (1974) 'Realism and the Cinema: Notes on Some Brechtian Theses', *Screen* 15, 2, 7–27.

Mayne, J. (1990) *Woman at the Keyhole: Feminism and Women's Cinema*. Bloomington: Indiana University Press.

_____ (1993) *Cinema and Spectatorship*. London and New York: Routledge.

Mellen, J. (1974) *Women and their Sexuality in the New Film*. New York: Dell.

Mercer, K. (1994) *Welcome to the Jungle: New Positions in Black Cultural Studies*. London and New York: Routledge.

Metz, C. (1975) 'The Imaginary Signifier', *Screen*, 16, 2, 14–75.

_____ (1983) *Psychoanalysis and Cinema: The Imaginary Signifier*. London: Macmillan.

Millet, K. (1970) *Sexual Politics*. London: Virago.

Mitchell, J. (1974) *Psychoanalysis and Feminism*. London: Allen Lance.

Mitchell, J. and J. Rose (eds) (1982) *Feminine Sexuality: Jacques Lacan and the École Freudienne*. New York: W. W. Norton.

Modleski, T. (ed.) (1986) *Studies in Entertainment: Critical Approaches to Mass Culture*. Bloomington: Indiana University Press.

_____ (1991) 'Cinema and the Dark Continent: Race and Gender in Popular Film', in *Feminism without Women: Cultural and Criticism in a Post-feminist Age*. London and New York: Routledge, 115–34.

_____ (1994) *Loving with a Vengeance: Mass Produced Fantasies for Women*. London and New York: Routledge.

_____ (1999) *Old Wives' Tales: Feminist Re-Visions of Film and Other Fictions*. London: I. B. Tauris.

Montrelay, M. (1978) 'Inquiry into Femininity', *m/f*, 1, 83–102.

Morley, D. (1980a) 'Texts, Readers, Subjects', in S. Hall, D. Hobson, A. Lowe and P. Willis (eds) *Culture, Media, Language*. London: Hutchinson, 163–73.

_____ (1980b) *The Nationwide Audience*. London: BFI.

Morris, M. (1988) *The Pirate's Fiancée: Feminism, Reading, Postmodernism*. London: Verso.

Mulvey, L. (1975) 'Visual Pleasure and Narrative Cinema', *Screen*, 16, 3, 6–18.

____ (1979) 'Feminism, Film and the *Avant-Garde*', *Framework*, 10, 3–10.

____ (1989) 'British Feminist Film Theory's Female Spectators: Presence and Absence', and contribution to 'The Spectatrix', *Camera Obscura*, 20/21, 68–81, 249.

____ (1999) 'Afterthoughts on "Visual Pleasure and Narrative Cinema" inspired by King Vidor's *Duel in the Sun*, 1946' [1981], in S. Thornham (ed.) *Feminist Film Theory: A Reader*. New York: New York University Press, 122–30.

Neale, S. (1983) 'Masculinity as Spectacle', *Screen*, 24, 6, 2–16.

Pajaczkowska, C. and Young, L. (2000) 'Racism, Representation, Psychoanalysis (1992)', in E. A. Kaplan (ed.) *Feminism and Film*. Oxford: Oxford University Press, 356–74.

Parmar, P. (1990) 'Black Feminism: The Politics of Articulation', in J. Rutherford (ed.) *Identity: Community, Culture, Difference*. London: Lawrence and Wishart, 101–26.

____ (2000) 'That Moment of Emergence [1993]', in E. A. Kaplan (ed.) *Feminism and Film*. Oxford: Oxford University Press, 375–78.

Penley, C. (1985) 'Feminism, Film Theory and the Bachelor Machines', *m/f*, 10, 42–52.

Petro, P. (1989) *Joyless Streets: Women and Melodramatic Representation in Weimar Germany*. New Jersey: Princeton University Press.

____ (2002) *Aftershocks of the New: Feminism and Film History*. New Brunswick and London: Rutgers University Press.

Rabinovitz, L. (1990) 'Temptations of Pleasure: Nickelodeons, Amusement Parks, and the Sights of Female Sexuality', *Camera Obscura*, 23, 71–88.

____ (1998) *For the Love of Pleasure: Women, Movies, and Culture in Turn-of-the-Century Chicago*. New Brunswick, NJ and London: Rutgers University Press.

Radway, J. (1987) *Reading the Romance: Women, Patriarchy and Popular Literature*. London: Verso.

Rich, A. (1980) 'Compulsory Heterosexuality and Lesbian Existence', *Signs*, 5, 4, 631–60.

Rich, B. R. (1998) *Chick Flicks: Theories and Memories of the Feminist Film Movement*. North Carolina: Duke University Press.

Rivette, J. (1985) 'The Genius of Howard Hawks [1953]', in J. Hillier (ed.) *Cahiers du cinéma. 1950s: Neo-Realism, Hollywood, New Wave*. Massachusetts: Harvard University Press.

Riviere, J. (1986) 'Womanliness as a Masquerade, 1929', in V. Burgin, J. Donald and C. Kaplan (eds) *Formations of Fantasy*. London and New York: Routledge, 35–44.

Rodowick, D. N. (1991) *The Difficulty of Difference: Psychoanalysis, Sexual Difference and Film Theory*. London and New York: Routledge.

Rosenberg, J. (1983) *Women's Reflections: The Feminist Film Movement*. Ann Arbor: UMI Press.

Rose, J. (1988) *Sexuality in the Field of Vision*. London: Verso.

Rosen, M. (1973) *Popcorn Venus: Women, Movies and the American Dream*. New York: